Even Unto Death

MARGARET FORD

David C. Cook Publishing Co.

ELGIN, ILLINOIS—WESTON, ONTARIO

EVEN UNTO DEATH

American edition published by
David C. Cook Publishing Co.
850 N. Grove Ave., Elgin, IL 60120

Cover by Joe Van Severen

ISBN 0-89191-197-9

ISBN 0 551 00794 X
LC 79-66755

Printed in the U.S.A.

TO
MARY LUWUM

Acknowledgements

I should like to acknowledge the help of many collaborators who have shared with me their recollections of Janani Luwum and whose words I have made my own. In particular I would like to thank Mr Peter Abe; The Rev Trevor Beedell; The Rev Colin Buchanan; The Rev Canon Norman Campbell; Miss Phebe Cave Browne Cave; The Rev Patrick Dearnley; Miss Janet Evans; Miss Edith J. Jordan; The Rev Prebendary Hugh Jordan; The Rt Rev Festo Kivengere; The Rev Canon Maurice Lea; Mrs Janet Lea; Mrs Wilmay Le Grice; The Rev Professor John Mbiti; The Rev J. R. B. McDonald; The Rt Rev Melchisadek Otim; Mr Yusto Otunno; Dr Dennis Pain; The Rev Canon D. M. Paton; Dr Philip Potter; Mrs Sylvia Rice-Oxley; The Rt Rev J. K. Russell; The Rev Malcolm Scott; Mrs Thelma Scott; The Rt Rev Kenneth Sansbury; Mrs Joan Sugden; The Rt Rev Oliver Tomkins; The Rt Rev Lucian Usher Wilson.

I should also like to thank The Rev Wallace Boulton, John Wilkins and Sir John and Lady Lawrence without whose expertise this book could not have been written. And I am indebted to Mary Stuart for her description of the Baganda in chapter one, which comes from her book *Land of Promise* (Highway Press, 1957).

Margaret Ford

Contents

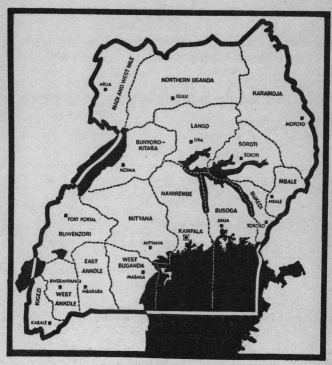

DIOCESES AND SEE TOWNS
OF THE CHURCH OF UGANDA

Therefore, my brothers, I implore you by God's mercy to offer your very selves to him: a living sacrifice, dedicated and fit for his acceptance, the worship offered by mind and heart. Adapt yourselves no longer to the pattern of this present world, but let your minds be remade and your whole nature thus transformed. Then you will be able to discern the will of God, and to know what is good, acceptable, and perfect . . .

Romans 12.1–2 NEB

1. Janani's Country

Janani Luwum, Archbishop of Uganda, Rwanda, Burundi and Boga-Zaire, killed some time during the evening of the 16th or the early hours of the 17th February, 1977, while in the hands of security forces in Uganda, proclaimed martyr a few days later, retraced the steps of the earlier Uganda martyrs. Boy pages at the court of the *kabaka*, or King of Buganda, they died with the name of Jesus on their lips.

Christianity had come to Uganda ten years before those first martyrs died. The Anglican Church Missionary Society had sent a small party of missionaries in 1877. Close on their heels, two years later in 1879, were a group of Roman Catholic White Fathers (Société des Missionaires d'Afrique). Alexander Mackay, a hot-headed Scot of the Church Missionary Society, and Fr Lourdel, his White Father rival, fought hard to plant the 'right kind' of Christianity in Uganda. It is surprising that this did not prevent a number of royal pages from being drawn to these uncompromising men. Eager groups of young boys, hungry for new knowledge, sat at the feet of Alexander Mackay, an engineer, in his newly established workshop, their eyes sparkling when he showed them his tools, the blacksmith's anvil and his printing press. Others of their number were attracted to Fr Lourdel, and gathered in groups in his tent nearby. Their questions were many. 'Tell us more about this man Jesus of whom you speak. Who is he? What is he like?' Many of them transferred their loyalty, their allegiance, to an even greater king than the *kabaka* – Jesus Christ, who became their new Lord and Master. There was no enmity between the two groups. They belonged to different branches of one family and loved each other. When King Mutesa died in 1884, still uncommitted to Christianity, the first baptisms had taken place.

Their new found faith in Jesus Christ was severely tested during the reign of the new *kabaka*, Mutesa's son Mwanga. Hostile to Christianity, in an effort to stamp out the new religion and bring his page boys to heel, he ordered the immediate arrest of a group of them who were on safari with Alexander Mackay.

The attack was so unexpected that the missionaries and their young converts were caught completely unawares. The boys, slightly ahead of the missionaries, suddenly found themselves surrounded by soldiers, who bound their hands with cord and marched them back to Mengo, the capital, while the missionaries were ordered home. Utterly confused, the missionaries tried to buy back the boys who had been captured by sending gifts of cloth to the *kabaka* and they warned the other boys at the mission to flee as quickly as possible. The gift secured the release of one boy who had been Mackay's servant. He hurried back with the terrible news that the other three had been condemned to be burned to death.

At the place of execution hundreds of people gathered. Some wept, others jeered, the parents of the boys pleaded with them, but they never wavered. They refused to denounce their new found faith in Jesus Christ, their Risen Lord and Master. Instead they burst into song, Baring-Gould's hymn of praise of the joys of heaven, which they made their own: 'Daily, daily sing the praises of the City God hath made . . .'

Little Yusufu, the youngest, who was only eleven years old, pleaded: 'Please don't cut off my arms. I will not struggle in the fire that takes me to Jesus.'

After this first outbreak of violence the number of baptisms increased, rather than decreased. Although attendance at the missions was forbidden, Christians would creep out of the court and steal down in ones and twos under cover of darkness. It was difficult for the missionaries to refuse the repeated requests of those who came at the peril of their lives, time after time, asking for baptism. Both missions were forced to reduce the length of time required for instruction. They baptised dozens of boys from the court and others who sought to follow Christ.

The first Catholic martyr was Joseph Mukasa Balikuddembe, a senior page. One of Mwanga's favourites, he was a powerful figure at court. Joseph was appalled when he heard of Mwanga's decision to kill the newly appointed Anglican Bishop, James Hannington. He rebuked Mwanga, saying that Mutesa, his father, would never have done such a thing, and that he would have to answer to God for it.

Mwanga now turned his anger and suspicions against Balikuddembe, accusing him of plotting with Fr Lourdel to kill him and for inciting the pages to refrain from homosexual practices common in court life. Balikuddembe's chief rival took advantage of Mwanga's threat of execution, and ordered him to be bound. The executioners were not in a hurry. Often Mwanga changed his mind when his temper cooled. But the rival had no intention of allowing Balikuddembe to escape. He sent messengers with strict orders to see that the execution was carried out immediately. Before he died, Joseph turned to his executioner and said : 'Tell Mwanga that I have been wrongly accused and unjustly condemned, but he has my forgiveness. However, unless he repents of this deed I shall be his accuser before the judgement seat of God.' His body was still burning on the fire when the expected reprieve arrived.

The storm which had been brewing underneath the surface finally broke towards the end of May 1886. One day Mwanga returned unexpectedly from an unsuccessful hippopotamus hunt to find most of the pages missing. They were in small groups, studying the Scriptures, unaware of his return. Mwanga's anger boiled over.

Both missions feared an all-out purge. Small groups of Christians, meeting in different places, spent the night praying and encouraging one another with words from St Matthew's Gospel which had been translated into their vernacular and printed by Mackay : 'Everyone who acknowledges me before men, I also will acknowledge before my Father who is in heaven' (10.32); and 'Blessed are those who are persecuted for righteousness' sake, for theirs is the kingdom of heaven' (5.4).

This time Mwanga's wrath did not blow itself out. He summoned his chiefs and blamed them for the disobedience of the pages. 'The boys have been bewitched by the Christians,' replied the chiefs. Anxious to save their own lives, they promised to find him better servants if he killed the boys.

9

The boys were quickly assembled before Mwanga and the chiefs and ordered to separate themselves into two groups – those who followed Christ, and those who followed Mwanga. So many of them claimed to be Christians that Mwanga hesitated to kill them all. He began to pick out first one, then another at random. The condemned prisoners were fastened together in pairs to prevent them from escaping. Each was asked for what charge he stood condemned. 'For following Christ,' they each replied. Orders were given for the long death march to the execution site at Namagongo, twenty-two miles from Mwanga's court at Mengo.

It took several days to collect enough firewood to burn all the victims. Eventually on 3rd June, 1886, everything was ready. The boys were tied carefully in reed matting, Catholics and Anglicans together, and placed in the centre of huge fires. The signal was given. The fires were lit. But instead of the usual wailing and screaming, only the crackling of the fires and the sounds of quiet sobbing, prayers and singing broke the stillness. The only person who wailed was the executioner. He had been forced to kill his own son, one of the Christian pages who died in the fire.

Louise Pirouet, in her book about the Ugandan martyrs, *Strong in the Faith*, writes:

> And they had faith in the establishment of a new era which they would not live to see. Bishop Hannington told his executioners that many would pass along the road which he had purchased with his life without let or hindrance to bring the Gospel to Uganda. And I believe the Ugandan martyrs also died in the hope of a new future, for 'faith is the assurance of things hoped for, the conviction of things not seen'.

Janani had that same faith and he, too, died in the hope of a new future.

The witness of the martyrs was one strand in Janani's inheritance. Another was the traditional rivalry between the Catholics and Anglicans in Uganda.

In the first days of the two churches in Uganda, when to be a Christian was to court death, the Anglican and Catholic missions held together wonderfully. They gave shelter to each other's converts; comforted one another. Anglicans and Catholics died together in the fire. Later on, united Anglican and Catholic forces succeeded in driving out the Arab Muslims from the court when they tried to assert control.

Uganda, a land-locked country with no access to the sea, has always been easy prey for invading armies and influences. Conscious of their vulnerability, influential Baganda, nurtured so carefully by the English CMS missionaries and the French White Fathers, began to look for some kind of European protection to stave off the Arabs, who often came as slave raiders. The Catholics looked towards France, the Anglicans towards England. England and France were traditional enemies, as well as traditional strongholds of Anglicanism and Catholicism. Rivalry and an intolerance of each other's theology which had always lurked beneath the surface burst into the open. There is evidence of this in Mackay's diary when he recorded the martyrdom of Joseph Balikuddembe: 'This fine tall lad has been a faithful servant of Mwanga ever since he became King. Formerly he read with me . . . afterwards the Catholics got hold of him.'

However, it was industrial and commercial development gathering momentum in Britain just before the turn of the century which sent British traders to Africa in search of raw materials. Captain Lugard of the British East Africa Company, afterwards Lord Lugard, and the first Anglican Bishop to take up residence in Uganda, Alfred Tucker, arrived together. Soon after his arrival Bishop Tucker wrote that Uganda in December 1890 was like a volcano on the verge of eruption. On the second Sunday after his arrival, a shot was heard during the service. Immediately the whole congregation sprang to its feet, arms were seized, and a rush made to the open space outside the mission. It was all about nothing. But the English and French parties, for parties they now have to be called, had worked themselves into a state of hysterical mistrust. Captain Lugard was encamped with a small body of men on the little hill known as Old Kampala, within sight of Mengo and of the newly built Anglican church on Namirembe Hill and the Roman Catholic mission on Rubaga. He had been ordered to keep the peace. With a troop of only a hundred armed men, he was encamped between the two contending parties.

Bishop Tucker offered to intervene. He placated the Catholic chiefs and peace was restored, but not for long. Fighting broke out continually during the next few years. Eventually, in 1894, Uganda was declared a British Protectorate. The presence of the British stemmed the encroachment of the Muslims and persuaded the 'French' and the 'English' to reach a compromise. But the deep wounds they inflicted on each other have never completely healed and they have been at war in their hearts for most of the time since. Both denominations, Catholic and Anglican, spread with vigour but in a most intense spirit of competition. Where one opened a school and built a church, the other sought to do so. The pattern of twin hills within sight of each other, each with a complex of church buildings, was copied all over Uganda.

However, there has been a great improvement in the last fifteen years or so. Pope John and the Second Vatican Council have played their part in this but there has been movement from the other side, too. The first Archbishop of Uganda, Dr Leslie Brown, subsequently Bishop of St Edmundsbury and Ipswich, had been a distinguished missionary in South India before he came to Uganda in 1953. Both in his time with the Church of South India and in Uganda, he did much to reconcile opponents and make them understand each other.

Another strand in Janani's inheritance was tribal. Within Uganda are flat savannah plains, rolling hills and rugged mountain peaks, and people belonging to two very different tribal groups, generally known as the Bantu and the Nilotes. Broadly speaking the south of Uganda is Bantu and the north is Nilotic. Janani was one of the Nilotic people. And he was proud of it. He attributed the strength of these warrior tribes to their preference for millet and meat. 'That is why we are so big and strong,' he would say. There was an unspoken comparison with the Bantu in the south, who are not warriors and eat *matoke*, the fruit of the plaintain.

The people called the Nilotes had migrated southwards down the Nile into the Sudan, where the first group, the Dinka, the Nuer, the Shilluk and the Anuak, settled. Another group, the Acholi, the Alur, and the Langi, settled on the savanna plains of northern Uganda, the Jo-Paluo in the eastern part of the country. A third group, scattered between the Nilo-Hamites and the Bantu, consists chiefly of the Kenyan and the Tanzanian Luos on the shores of lake Victoria.

While the Nilotes traditionally are warriors and hunters, the more sophisticated Bantu are agricultural people grouped together in four separate and highly organised kingdoms, Buganda, Toro, Ankole and Bunyoro. Buganda, from which Uganda took its name, is the largest and most dominant. In the language of the Bantu peoples, meaning is changed by prefixes. Buganda is the province of Uganda which is inhabited by the Baganda who speak Luganda. One Bagandan is a Muganda. The British administrators were charmed with Buganda. Situated on the Equator, at an altitude of 4,000 feet, it was neither too hot nor too cold. The sun shone every day. Gentle rain all the year round encouraged rapid growth, so that lush vegetation clothed the undulating hills. The admiration of the British for this green and pleasant land was matched by an equal admiration for its people. They were impressed by these proud, chocolate coloured natives with their exquisite manners. In the homes of the upper classes, highly dressed skins and beautifully made mats lay stretched out on the floor, giving an air of comfort and taste. Visitors were offered *mbisi*, a drink made from the juice of ripe bananas, in little golden coloured gourds, placed on a tiny mat of red bark cloth and covered with a deliciously fresh banana leaf. Then there was music. Beautifully made harps were plucked on all the roads round Mengo. Every goatherd had his own flute. The Baganda looked so attractive dressed in their beautiful terra-cotta coloured barkcloth. Their hunger for knowledge, their readiness to accept new ideas, their ability to read and write quickly and accurately amazed the first British administrators. Furthermore, the established kingdom of Buganda with its hierarchical system of chiefs, was an ideal foundation for the orderly government introduced by the British Administration. The Baganda were apt pupils and they soon became excellent civil servants.

Bishop Tucker was also impressed by the eagerness of the Baganda to feed on the living word of God. Often, early in the morning, he was aroused from peaceful slumber by the murmur of voices as a continuous stream of people flowed past his house, climbing Namirembe Hill on their way to church, at that time not a very grand building, just built of timber, reeds and grass. Bishop Tucker was a man of tremendous drive and missionary vision who looked forward to an indigenous church in Uganda.

It was from Buganda that the good news of the gospel was taken to the other tribes. Baganda Christians went out from Namirembe, their headquarters, with CMS missionaries for whom they acted as interpreters. The Baganda and the missionaries preached the gospel of Christ together. Partnership in mission was established in Uganda before the turn of the century. Wherever they went people responded to the message of the gospel. Bishop Tucker's vision of a self-governing, self-expanding, self-financing church began to be realised as small churches were built up under local leadership all over the country.

Neither the British administrators nor the missionaries found it easy to penetrate the vast northern region of Uganda, the home of the Nilotic people. The Nilotes have no strong affiliation one with another. Each particular tribe comprises different chiefdoms. Each chiefdom has many clans and each clan has many families. Groups of related families live together in a village. The clans were often at war with one another; enmity and a warring spirit were the natural order of the day.

Janani's home was in East Acholi, on the borders of the Sudan. This area remained untouched much longer than any other, with perhaps the exception of Karamoja in north-eastern Uganda, because communication and travel is so difficult. The climate is less favourable too, and the landscape less picturesque. Acres of burnt scrubland are not pleasing to the eye. The Nilotes burn the bush at the end of the dry season to encourage tender blades of green grass which shoot up after the first heavy showers of the rains for the benefit of their herds of cattle. The roads are often impassable in the rainy season and dusty and uncomfortable in the dry season. The present bridge over the River Nile at Kabalega Falls was opened only in 1951 and Gulu, the administrative centre of West Acholi, has only been linked to Kampala, Uganda's capital, by tarmac road since 1971. The tarmac ends at Gulu. Kitgum, the administrative centre of East Acholi, is still, even today, connected to the rest of Uganda by a *murram* road. *Murram* is hard-packed red earth.

The British did not find the Nilotes as attractive as the Bantu. At first they were repelled by these fierce, immensely tall, unwashed natives, wearing animal skins, who leaped about flourishing spears. The Nilotes are proud, proud of their strength, their staying power, their prowess in battle. The British administrators soon recognised these qualities and recruited large numbers of them in their army.

Bishop Tucker, however, saw that their fierce exterior hid an eager, enquiring mind. But you had to be tough to survive in Acholi. Disease was rife, the heat intense. Bishop Tucker had to withdraw the missionaries from the region in 1908 because many had become ill. It took a week to get to the nearest doctor.

From these small beginnings the church in Acholi took root and began to grow. But its roots were shallow. *Dini*, the word used to describe the new religion the missionaries taught, was only associated with 'reading'. The Acholi quickly recognised that reading and learning how to speak English were of obvious and immediate practical value. But *dini* did not impinge on clan ritual which is centred round the spirits who are called *jogi*, the *ajwaka* (clan ritual expert) and the *abila* (clan ritual shrine) around which Acholi life revolved.

The first missionaries measured the initial impact of Christianity on Acholi society by the number of readers and the amount of money collected voluntarily for the work of the church. There were, in those early days, many readers, and money flowed in. In the early 1930s three permanent church buildings were erected in the administrative centres of Gulu, Kitgum and Lira. Janani was one of the many young boys who helped to build the church at Kitgum. Schools were built. The Acholi were eager to learn the 'three Rs' – reading, writing and arithmetic – and more than happy to receive all the fruits of development that *dini* and the British administrators brought them.

On the other hand, comparatively few men and women were prepared to make a complete break from the animist practices of clan ritual and begin a new life in the service of Jesus Christ with the total commitment that this required. But those who did experience Christ's transforming power, tended to become natural Christian leaders as they grew up in an environment which showed scant regard even for their traditional animist faith. The *abila* shrines may have been neglected, but they did not disappear. Nor did the *ajwaka* go out of business. Rather, the British administrator, the missionary and the *ajwaka* walked unwittingly hand in hand together as they sought to minister to the spiritual and physical needs of the Acholi. Their critics would say that the Acholi like to have a foot in every camp but the exceptions to this rule, if rule it be, may be more significant for the future than their present numbers would signify. Men who stand as Christians in Acholi — men like Janani — stand firm.

2. Childhood and Early Life

Janani, an Acholi, was a typical Nilotic. Tall, jet black, he was a giant of a man.

He was born in 1922, at Mucwini in East Acholi, close to the border of the Sudan. The family homestead, a cluster of grass-thatched mud huts, is set amid arid savannah plains dissected by river beds. During the rainy season these river beds are impassable as torrents of water pour down them. But during the dry season water is a scarce commodity, drawn from scattered bore holes and carried in large earthenware pots balanced precariously on the heads of women and girls who often cover long distances each day in search of it.

The Acholi, both men and women, are energetic, hard-working people. Each member of the family has a job to do. Janani's responsibility in those early days was herding the family's cattle, goats and sheep. Herding cattle is not unpleasant – unless the shepherd loses one of his animals. Boys who fail to tether securely the sheep and goats in their care, and allow them to stray into a neighbour's field, receive a thorough beating. Goats are expert nibblers of succulent new maize plants and by customary law the owner has to pay a fine if his animals damage his neighbour's crops.

Boys of his age loved Janani. He soon became their leader in all their activities. They roamed the savannah plains; stalked wild animals; climbed trees. Janani was a skilled marksman. All Acholi boys from an early age carry a catapult and quickly learn to shoot small birds to supplement the family diet. Later on they graduate to a bow and arrow. In traditional dancing Janani was one of the best in Mucwini. He could play the *lukeme*, a locally made musical instrument, and the drum. When he was older he became an instructor in the local music. The Acholi are famous throughout Uganda for their dancing and their fame reached London in coronation year, 1953, when a team of dancers from East Acholi danced the *bwola* (the royal dance) before the Queen.

East Acholi has a beauty all its own, though not immediately recognisable when you are confronted for the first time with stunted acacia trees, bare thorn bushes and miles upon miles of long grass. But in Acholi it is not the beauty of the landscape that matters. It is the clouds that are important, how they are gathering in the sky and whether rain is on the way. Acholi is blessed with an abundance of rain, but not too much from April to October. When the rainy season approaches, the men gather together and go to open one another's new sim-sim, groundnut or millet fields. Land is no problem in Acholi; new fields are opened every year. Since they are traditionally hunters, the Acholi only clear sufficient land to feed their own families. The women and girls are responsible for the planting, weeding and harvesting of the crops.

Acholi women are generally tough, hard-working and persistent. Janani's mother was no exception. She is still alive today and a tremendous force within the family. The land around their homestead was fertile. The family never went hungry. The earthenware cooking pot, perched on the traditional fire between three large stones, was seldom empty, and there was always chicken for the visitor.

Eliya Okello, Janani's father, was an early convert to Christianity. He was a dedicated man who had committed his life to serving the Lord as a church teacher. 'I could never understand,' Janani would say, 'why, one Christmas, my father gave our *only* cow to the church ... I found out later, though, when I gave *my* life to Christ, surrendered all to him.'

Money was scarce. Church teachers received very little pay. Janani was ten years old before there was money available to give him the opportunity of attending school. But once in school he quickly made up for lost time. After primary school he was admitted to Gulu High School. He often spoke of how he walked to and from Gulu, a distance of eighty miles, at the beginning and end of term.

His family looked forward to the day when he would

become a chief and play an important part in the new world. Surely, at this stage, Janani also aspired to be a chief.

After he left school, because the money ran out, he joined Boroboro teacher training college, based on the small mission station five miles from Lira, the administrative centre of Lango district. Although he came from a Christian home and attended a missionary training college, he was not at this time a converted Christian. Nevertheless, he began to show signs of leadership and display a brand of courage that is required of those who pull against the tide.

On one occasion the students staged a strike, complaining of poor food and not enough salt. A CMS woman missionary, Phebe Cave Browne Cave, was temporarily in charge of the college and the students, mostly men, resented this. It was Janani who persuaded them to drop their complaints. They should support the staff, he said, especially the acting principal, who was trying to help them with their studies. Somehow he made them all agree and the meeting ended happily with much laughter.

One of Janani's best friends at the college was Peter Abe, a member of staff. Janani was in his second year when Peter Abe married in 1942. The marriage ceremony and tea party were successfully arranged and organised by him although he was only about twenty years of age. The most striking feature of the wedding arrangements was the one hundred yard canopy arch of papyrus constructed by the students.

In the class, Janani was always top or at least amongst the first three. He was a talented artist and excelled in stick drawings which are so important in blackboard illustrations. In Peter Abe's rating and final assessment he was given the highest grade in practical teaching. This assessment was sent to the education department in Kampala, who doubted its correctness. Three experts were sent to verify and ratify it.

They really tested Janani. He was required to teach a prepared lesson in the lower primary and an extempore lesson in the upper primary. He was also required to run two physical education lessons simultaneously, as can happen in schools when one of the masters is sick. Janani proved equal to the task. He organised the group by giving them Acholi games which made each group work almost independently with very little supervision. He was first class on the blackboard; his drawings of the biblical story during the religious knowledge lesson were superbly vivid. There was nothing the panel of examiners could do but confirm and endorse the assessment.

Outside in the field he soon commanded the respect of those with whom he worked or stayed. Never personally ambitious, he preferred to work loyally under anyone put above him. In his home region he commanded the greatest respect, which was difficult to achieve among the Acholi.

It was while he was working as a school teacher that he became a Christian. He had graduated from the teacher training college in 1942 and had been posted to Puranga primary school in East Acholi.

Janani came to the Lord on January 6th, 1948, at half past noon, in his own home village, through the preaching of Yusto Otunno and his wife Josephine, members of the *balokole*. The word *balokole* comes from the Luganda word meaning 'saved ones', and this East African revival movement swept through the church like a raging bush fire in the late 1930s. The Holy Spirit took hold of men and women, many of whom had faithfully attended and supported the church for years, opened their eyes and laid bare their hearts. Suddenly people began to see that their Christianity had been nominal and that their lives had been dominated by the sins of pride, hatred, debauchery, drunkenness, division and shallow commitment. They openly confessed their sins and called on others to rouse themselves from their former complacency, to choose between life with Christ or death with the devil, to 'walk in the light', and to allow the blood of Christ to cleanse and save them from their sins. Many people responded in tears to this fiery message of repentance. Men who had been living with more than one wife came forward, confessed, married one wife in church, and provided for the others. Those who had stolen their neighbour's cows returned them. They burned their charms and poured away their local beer. These 'brethren' were known and still are known as *balokole*. Just as the first Baganda Christians moved out of Namirembe to tell others about Christ, the *balokole* were convicted by the Holy Spirit to leave the narrow confines of their churches, and also move out to warn others to repent, to choose Jesus and be saved by his cleansing blood.

It was to this movement that Yusto Otunno and his wife Josephine belonged. Yusto had written to Janani and the other Christians in the village to let them know of their intention to hold a mission there. On their arrival, Janani's father, Eliya Okello, and the other Christians welcomed them in the name of Jesus Christ. During the preaching Janani felt convicted; twice he broke out in a heavy sweat. When this happened a third time he confessed Jesus Christ as his Lord and in tears repented of his sins, crying aloud before God and men, so that the villagers came running to see what was happening.

Janani asked Otunno and his wife to pray for him, that the Lord would lead him, and protect him from 'backsliding'. At the end of the meeting Janani gave his testimony. He told the people: 'Today I have become a leader in Christ's army. I am prepared to die in the army of Jesus. As Jesus shed his blood for the people, if it is God's will, I will do the same.'

They tied a piece of cloth on their doorpost to show that the Holy Spirit had entered the house and triumphed over Satan. During the meeting Janani's father had sat quietly on one side. Suddenly he jumped up, just before the prayers. With tears in his eyes he confessed that although he was a Christian, there was still sin in his life. He went into his house. A few minutes later he returned carrying two locally made pipes of tobacco. He broke them in two and burned the tobacco to show the people gathered around that he had put away those things which were not acceptable to his saviour, Jesus Christ. Twelve people accepted Christ as their saviour and master that day, eight of them members of Eliya's family, including Aloni Okecho, Janani's brother.

Janani and his family escorted Otunno and his wife a distance of six miles to their home. On the way they praised God singing:

Tukutendereza Yesu,	Glory, glory, hallelujah!
Yesu Mwana gw'endiga:	Glory, glory to the Lamb!
Omusaayi gwo gunaazizza;	Oh, the cleansing blood has reached me!
Nkwebaza Mulokozi.	Glory, glory to the Lamb.

21

Later on Janani tended to keep his conversion experience to himself. But in December 1976 he told a theological student and his wife that some people in the Deliverance Church, a new charismatic revivalist movement, thought he had not experienced the Holy Spirit in a dramatic way. The truth, he said, was different: 'When I was converted, after realising that my sins were forgiven and the implications of Jesus' death and resurrection, I was overwhelmed by a sense of joy and peace. I suddenly found myself climbing a tree to tell those in the school compound to repent and turn to Jesus Christ. From time to time I spoke in tongues. I stayed up that tree for a long time. Later on I discovered that some boys were converted due to a sermon I preached up that tree. The reality of Jesus overwhelmed me – and it still does. But I would be wrong to demand that those who are converted should climb a tree and speak in tongues.'

After this conversion experience Janani was caught up for a whole year with the revival movement and involved personally in its struggle with the church. He was dismissed from one church school by the church authorities who accused him of spoiling the pupils with his message of 'repentance'. Revival was painful and costly. It ripped the church from top to bottom, since many church leaders saw the revival movement as divisive. It is not always comfortable to 'walk in the light' constantly with your neighbour, nor to meet face to face brethren on fire with an uncompromising love of the Lord.

Less than a month after his conversion, in February 1948, Janani was arrested with eight others and brought before the sub-chief of Mucwini, charged with disturbing the peace. At an open-air meeting Janani had emphasised the sins of drunkenness and of smoking, which in that situation was associated with excessive drinking. He challenged his hearers to choose between Christ and the devil; life or death; urging them to repent of their sins, and spend their time with Christ and his followers listening to God's word, rather than with the devil and his followers drinking and smoking. The arrests had been contrived by the church teachers who seldom spoke out against drunkenness, but preferred to turn a blind eye to what was going on around them.

The following morning they were taken to Kitgum, the

administrative centre of East Acholi, thrown in prison, tortured and given no food for two days. The prison warders repeatedly asked them to denounce their faith but Janani replied on their behalf: 'You are good people and our beloved brothers. It is not you, but your master, Satan, who is using you to torture us and leave us to go hungry. We love you, and our master, Jesus Christ, loves you too. The wooden bars at the window of this tiny cell cannot separate us from the love of God, nor stop us proclaiming his message of salvation, through his son Jesus Christ. All of us here are committed to Christ, even unto death.'

The brethren rejoiced and praised the Lord that they had been counted worthy to suffer for Christ's sake. After a short while they were released. All of them returned to their own homes, stronger in faith, and even more committed to preaching repentance.

On another occasion, Yusto Otunno, and Janani's brother, Aloni Okecho, were arrested. Janani was in court when they appeared before the magistrate and was greatly concerned when he saw that Otunno had been badly beaten. He stood up and addressed the court: 'Have these people been beaten,' he asked, 'because they have been preaching in the name of Jesus Christ?' He continued: 'I am one of the *balokole* myself.'

Janani's bold statement embarrassed the magistrate, who promptly ordered his arrest for contempt of court. He was sentenced to a month's imprisonment with the option of a twenty shillings fine. Janani would have preferred to go to jail and suffer alongside his fellow brethren but they implored him to pay the fine and continue preaching the message of salvation during their temporary enforced absence. Yusto and Aloni served their sentence; and through their ministry in prison seventy prisoners came to Christ.

The *balokole* did not give up, nor were they discouraged by opposition, imprisonment, ridicule, or false allegations. They continued to travel together in groups all over East Acholi, preaching the message of salvation to all who cared to listen. They praised God in all circumstances, 'walked in the light', and admonished each other.

On a hot Sunday afternoon in November 1948, Janani preached to a group of brethren on the compound of All Saints' Church in Kitgum. Tears streaming down his face, he said: 'The Spirit of the Lord has shown me that many educated men have run away from the church. They want the church to fall, and to fall alone. Today, I promise before God and all of you assembled here, that if the church is falling, she will fall on me. I surrender myself to the church.' He fell on the ground and wept, amid loud shouts of praise and thanksgiving.

As time went on the church leaders grew more and more suspicious of the *balokole* teaching on repentance. They tried repeatedly to halt the revival movement by going to the government and accusing its members of disturbing the peace – but without result. The movement continued to gather momentum and there was the added danger that it could easily become a breakaway sect.

Shortly after Janani's outburst on the compound of All Saints' Church, Otunno shared with him an idea that one of the brethren who had been educated should join the full-time ministry of the church. In this way they would be better placed to preach salvation within the church and at the same time challenge its leaders with the necessity to repent and be saved by the cleansing blood of Christ. The brethren warmed to the idea. They turned to Janani and asked him to sacrifice his teaching career and offer himself for the ministry.

Janani knew that his family wanted him to be a chief. They were expecting it of him. But he knew in his heart that God was calling him to forsake all, to be a pastor – a shepherd.

3. Apprenticeship

And so Janani became a pastor of the Anglican Church in Uganda. He did so through a new course pioneered by Bishop Usher Wilson of the diocese of the Upper Nile, of which Acholi was a part. The bishop had been looking for suitable men to be future church leaders. Previously, they had had to go through a series of courses before attending a two-year lay readers' course at Buwalasi Theological College. All these courses had been in Luganda, the language of the Baganda. This caused difficulties for the men from the northern part of Uganda, for it was a language they neither spoke nor understood.

The bishop therefore proposed a lay readers' course in English for bright, eager young men who had a good command of it. This idea was bitterly opposed by the missionaries and many of the pastors in his diocese since they felt it would undermine the growth of an indigenous African church. But Bishop Usher Wilson refused to drop the idea. He found his young men, and Janani Luwum was one of them. With John Wasikye, now Bishop of Mbale, and Akis Wesonga, now secretary of the United Bible Society, Janani joined the first lay readers' course conducted in English at Buwalasi Theological College.

He arrived there in January 1949, leaving his wife Mary and their first-born, a three-year-old daughter, at home in the village, having placed them under the care of Yusto Otunno. Mary joined him a year later. Janani always spoke of Buwalasi, with its wonderful views of Mount Elgon, as one of the most beautiful places in Uganda. Mary found it cold in the early mornings when the mist clung to the mountains before the sun illuminated the distant peaks. At times she felt an alien, caught in between these mountains, living among people who spoke a different language, ate different food (the despised *matoke*) and practised different customs. Then she would long with all her heart to return to the hot, dry savannah plains, to the traditional, familiar ways of her people. But she and Janani were together. For Janani that was all that mattered. At Buwalasi he learnt to live with tensions – the tension between the old and the new, between the traditional and the modern – first of all within his own family.

After a miscarriage, Mary bore him a second child, a son. They called him Benoni, meaning 'son of sorrow'. Acholi names are an outward expression of feeling and tell of the circumstances surrounding the birth.

At the end of 1950 Janani and Mary left Buwalasi and returned home to Acholi. Janani was attached to St Philip's Church in Gulu as a lay reader and he also taught the catechists at the archdeaconry training centre.

Mary kept their small house behind Gulu High School compound very neatly. Janani had a talent for making things – chicken houses were his speciality. On one occasion he found an old oil drum which he earmarked for storing water. He was undeterred when he cut his chest with a flying sliver of steel whilst removing the top. He had to go to hospital to have the sliver removed. But he treated it all as a joke.

He attacked all his work with similar vigour. He helped with translation at deanery meetings, encouraged sub-grade school teachers, organised the children's services at St Philip's, fostered the growth of Sunday Schools and organised camps for secondary school boys who helped with the building of new classrooms and churches constructed from grass.

Bishop Usher Wilson was thrilled with his protégé. Janani, he felt, had fully justified his faith in the rising generation. But his older clergy were still very sceptical of these bright young men who spoke fluent English and thought they knew all the answers. The pastor of St Philip's, Canon Latigo, did not readily endorse his bishop's decision to accept Janani for a further three-year course at Buwalasi Theological College leading to ordination.

Janani returned to Buwalasi at the beginning of 1953 with his wife and family, successfully completed his ordination course and was ordained deacon by the newly appointed bishop of Northern Uganda, Keith Russell, on St Thomas's Day, 21st December, 1955. The following year, 1956, Bishop Usher Wilson ordained him as a priest.

Both these bishops had pondered deeply how to promote Ugandan leaders in the church. When Bishop Russell went home to England on leave in 1957, he shared his thoughts on this subject with many but in particular with the congregation of St Mary's, Shortlands, in Kent. The vicar, the Rev Neville Sugden, asked the bishop if he had anyone in mind who would benefit from a year's course in England. The name that sprang immediately to the bishop's mind was Janani's.

The congregation of St Mary's readily agreed to raise sufficient money to cover Janani's fare to England so that he could attend a one-year course at St Augustine's College, Canterbury. At that time, St Augustine's was the central college of the Anglican Communion, and helped to train many priests and laymen who were subsequently called to high office in the Anglican family of churches.

So in due course, after arrangements had been made for his family's welfare during his absence, Janani arrived in London, one bleak grey day in January 1958. He was wearing a thin grey suit, but he soon acquired a large black overcoat and a thick woollen cardigan from Marks and Spencer.

Now he had to meet new challenges as he came face to face with the rich variety of Anglican traditions that had found a place in the life of the college. He enjoyed the weekly get-together in the Gateway Chamber when some question of theological importance and practical concern would be discussed. On one occasion, in the course of discussion, the warden, Dr Kenneth Sansbury, explained what the German Protestant theologian Rudolf Bultmann meant by his call to demythologise the Bible. At first, Janani was shocked, but as the session continued he began to see that, whether one accepted Bultmann or not, he had raised a fundamental question: how do you interpret a gospel given in a particular cultural context so that it becomes relevant to the people of another culture? It was a question which Christians from Africa and Asia had to face, as well as Europeans.

On another occasion, during a course of ecumenical lectures, a visiting Baptist scholar set out the case for believers' baptism. Janani was again shocked, but this time he could find no value in the view presented to him. 'For us in Africa,' he said, 'the family is a unit. It would be unthinkable for the parents to be baptised and the children left behind.' Later, however, when he was back in Uganda, two who supported believers' baptism were struck by his gentleness and lack of dogmatism when they challenged his views. He admitted he had never asked himself why he baptised infants and said he would think about the matter seriously. He continued: 'We say we have four million baptised Christians, but in reality where are they? Can we really say in all seriousness that there are four million Anglicans in Uganda who have died with Christ and are living in the power of his risen life? Are these members on the baptismal register or are they members in reality?' Perhaps his experience at St Augustine's may have helped him to face the question of infant baptism with an open mind.

Janani returned to Uganda in 1959. Everyone said he would do well. They considered it a foregone conclusion. Had he not received the benefits of theological training in England? To see what he would make of it, Bishop Russell posted him to what he considered the worst parish in his diocese.

At the end of the 1950s Uganda was developing rapidly. The economy was booming. There was an atmosphere of joyous expectancy. The country felt proud at having received Britain's stamp of approval, so that there would be no bloody struggle for independence.

But life for Janani was not so happy. He soon found himself floundering in the parish of Lira Palwo in East Acholi. The parish was forty miles wide, with twenty-four daughter churches, yet his only means of transport was a bicycle. It would be unfair to attribute his apparent failure at Lira Palwo to personal defects. He was beginning his parochial ministry at a time when the church in Northern Uganda found herself ill-prepared for the political fervour which reached the northern part of the country in 1958.

The party divisions were based on the division between the churches, so that the Democratic Party was mainly

Catholic and the **Uganda People's Congress** was mainly Protestant. The competition between these parties fitted perfectly with the traditions of clan and chiefdom competition and enmity. The Acholi, noted for their eloquence in argument, loved politics and enjoyed pinpointing fallacies in their opponent's arguments.

Undoubtedly the growth of the political parties played a significant part in the steady decline of Christianity in Acholi and Lango during the late fifties and sixties. The people's sudden infatuation with politics tested the validity of the church's very existence. Money and local leadership were no longer so readily forthcoming. Previously the church had enjoyed an absolute monopoly over money-giving : no other organisation asked for gifts, week by week, year by year. Suddenly political party workers started going round with the collecting bag and for the first time people in the villages had to choose – should they give to the party or to the church?

For the same reasons, local leadership was severely affected. Bishop Russell in his book *Men Without God* tells the story of one very strong branch of the Mothers' Union in a remote village in Northern Uganda. They built a new church, bought new altar cloths and helped the pastor with gifts of food. But in 1964 the church fell down, termites ate the altar cloths, and the pastor was transferred. The reason, writes Bishop Russell, was that Mrs O., of the Mothers' Union, had become the branch secretary of the Uganda People's Congress and had neither the time nor the enthusiasm for two jobs. Her party activities did not in any way make her hostile to the church : the church just got pushed out. There was no other leader in that village and the women who at Mrs O's bidding used to mud the walls of the church and cut grass for the roof now followed her in a new direction.

For Janani, Christ came first, the party second. But the gospel he proclaimed, one of total commitment to Christ, fell on stony ground in the parish of Lira Palwo. The people came willingly to pray and the grass thatched church was packed on Sunday mornings, but *dini* was now labelled in many people's minds as second class. Janani tried his best to encourage people to give their 'first fruits' to God but for the most part they remained unmoved, arguing that it was possible to support both the party and the church.

On one occasion he visited a family in his parish to try to encourage them to give to a special church appeal. The woman of the household did not refuse her support. She simply told him, 'I will bring my gift when I have sold my second grade cotton.' He did not thank the woman but quietly asked her how she would feel if God told her, 'This year the first rains will fall on your neighbour's fields but your fields will remain dry until the second rains.' The woman saw the point immediately; taking down a small pot, she removed a bundle of notes and handed them to him.

Janani was not the sort of man who gave up easily or ran away from a situation by asking for a transfer. Neither, on the other hand, was he immune from the acute depression, which sets in when you continually come up against a blank wall. Sometimes, very discouraged, he would talk at great length of how he had tried everything he could think of to encourage the people in the gospel of Christ – African traditional music in the services of worship, competitions in gift-giving, and a monthly news sheet to keep people in touch with what was happening. 'Whatever I do, it doesn't work. But here I am, I have a job to do, and I must do it.'

Mary, his wife, was a constant source of encouragement. Though usually in the background, she always supported him in his work. Pastors were supposed to receive sixty shillings a month but they rarely received their salary since it was calculated on a percentage basis of the total parish giving. Mary was a good farmer, hard working and diligent. There was always a warm welcome and food in the home.

For three years Janani remained in Lira Palwo without seeing any obvious fruits of his labours. On a number of occasions Bishop Russell considered taking him away from the parish, fearful that one day his depression would be the cause of his voluntary departure from the ministry. Later Janani was to say, 'They pulled me out of Lira Palwo too quickly.' There was always a note of sadness in his voice when he spoke about this period of his life.

But there were fruits. Benoni Ogwal was one of the young delinquents of the parish. On one occasion they burned down the church. But Benoni became a changed man: 'Janani's attitude to forgiveness helped me to surrender my life to Christ.' Benoni Ogwal is now Bishop of Northern Uganda, in exile in Canada.

4. Responsibility

In 1962, the year Uganda achieved full political independence, Janani became vice-principal of Buwalasi Theological College. These were stirring times. Internal self-government had come to Uganda the year before, with the Democratic Party under its leader Benedicto Kiwanuka in power. On 8th October, 1962, just before midnight, Ugandans, missionaries and other expatriate workers had joined hands round huge bonfires which were lit everywhere as the Union Jack was hauled down and Uganda's own flag was run up. Drums heralded a new future under the leadership of Dr Milton Obote, a Langi. His Uganda People's Congress Party, in alliance with the 'Kabaka only' party, had defeated the Democratic Party in the pre-Independence elections. Shortly afterwards Uganda was declared a Republic and the *kabaka*, the traditional King of Buganda, was chosen as its first President.

Now, for the second time, Janani left Uganda for England. He had been awarded a bursary to study for two years at the London College of Divinity. Like many other African students, he arrived with an elementary education on which had been crammed theological training under limited conditions. His ambitions and the expectations of those behind him were pitched very high. This meant work and plenty of it. With such an educational opportunity, he was in a hurry. People in a hurry, even when their motives are good, are apt to be abrupt with others. This could never be said of Janani, who loved and cared for people even more than learning.

He made many friends whilst he was in England. He spent all his vacations with Neville and Joan Sugden at Shortlands and entered fully into the life of the family, sharing its joys and sorrows. Joan Sugden told me, 'I can still see Janani, a big man in every way, saying to me, whilst

32

waving a tea-towel : 'Come along, mother, we will help with the drying-up.'

Throughout all his vacations, he worked very long hours at his books studying Hebrew and Greek. Neville and Joan Sugden were amazed at the demands he made on himself, without ever a word of self-pity or discontent. He was a true family man and their own young family of four adored him. He was always urging them along with their school work and was keen that they should work hard so as to get on and succeed and eventually join him in Uganda or offer themselves for full-time Christian service.

Mary joined him during his last term so she was able to share some of his experiences in England. They returned home in June 1965. Janani's hard work had reaped its reward. He had made the grade for the college diploma and was now an Associate of the London College of Divinity, having covered three years' work in two.

Back in Buwalasi, he took over as principal. The college was running down, because Bishop Tucker College had been chosen to serve as the provincial college, and church finances could not afford two top-level training centres. In a year or two Buwalasi would be closed.

Janani had always felt at home in Buwalasi and Mary was now more at ease there. She had become used to the people and their customs, and to the weather. England had been much colder, so in comparison Buwalasi was warm and the sun shone more often. Her elder daughter was a great help; three of the younger children were in primary school, leaving only two at home. Janani's family soon settled down in their pleasant bungalow, glad to be together again.

The community at Buwalasi was a happy one, and the staff team united though drawn from an immensely varied tribal spectrum. Janani's implicit trust in his staff and his happy partnership with his Mugandan vice-principal helped them all to see beyond tribal divisions.

He preached frequently to the staff and students, always with Christ at the centre. But at least one former member of staff recalls losing the sense of the sermon because of the magnetic attraction of Janani's facial expressions, especially when he gave a partial smile and a very pink tongue did a full sweep from one corner of his mouth to the other and back again.

His time at Buwalasi was short. In September 1966 he was asked to be Provincial Secretary. It was not an easy job. When he arrived in Namirembe he found himself at the tail-end of a furious row over the appointment of Dr Leslie Brown's successor as Archbishop. He had to find a way to soothe the injured feelings of the Baganda. It had seemed to them a foregone conclusion that their own Dr Dunstan Nsubuga, now Bishop of Namirembe, should be elected as the new Archbishop. Instead, they had to watch in disbelief as Erica Sabiti, to them an unknown Munyankole from south-west Uganda, was elected and installed as Archbishop in their own cathedral, St Paul's, Namirembe, in 1966.

The Baganda refused to accept Archbishop Sabiti's appointment and made life very difficult for him. Bishop Nsubuga would not vacate the Archbishop's official residence, and since there was no other house available on Namirembe Hill, nor an office, Archbishop Sabiti continued to live at Fort Portal, the headquarters of his own diocese of Ruwenzori. His health was soon severely affected since he found the frequent 200-mile journey to Kampala on a rough earth road very exhausting.

Janani, as Provincial Secretary, was given the formidable task of overcoming these difficulties, which he did in part by organising the building of the present Archbishop's house and provincial offices on Namirembe and by proposing a separate diocese of Kampala carved out of Namirembe. The latter idea was given an airing but did not come into effect until he became Bishop of Northern Uganda.

Although some of the practical difficulties were overcome, the Baganda were never reconciled in their hearts. The undignified departure of their beloved *kabaka* had dealt a second mortifying blow on the whole Baganda tribe which alienated them from Church and State. It was not altogether surprising that Dr Obote's partnership with the *kabaka* was short-lived and ended as it did, in May 1966, with the *kabaka* narrowly escaping with his life after the attack on his palace and seeking refuge with friends in England. Dr Obote seized the Presidency and democracy was thrown to the winds. He relied increasingly on his army to help him wield the power he needed to rule Uganda. He alienated the whole of the Baganda tribe. He was afraid to travel in Buganda without an armed escort. But always at the back of his mind was the comforting thought that his army contained large numbers of his own fellow Langi and Acholi tribesmen and he knew he could count on their loyalty if the Baganda tried to take control.

Another irritant to the Baganda was the Bikangaga Report, published in 1969, proposing the establishment of Church Commissioners to hold all church land on behalf of the province. The diocese of Namirembe owned more land than all other dioceses put together, and so the Baganda were particularly suspicious of the proposal, since they immediately concluded that the provincial administration intended to 'eat' their land and swallow them up.

But in spite of the difficulties of division, the Church of Uganda was determined to grow and move forward. In January 1967 the Ten Year Plan had been presented to members of the provincial assembly, meeting in Kampala. Janani's own enthusiasm for the Ten Year Plan enabled him to enthuse others. It embodied Bishop Tucker's vision of a self-governing, self-expanding and self-financing church. The Church of Uganda had already achieved the first two but as yet was not self-financing. The plan proposed that by the time the church came to celebrate its centenary, in 1977, the administration should have been completely overhauled, the laity should have been mobilised and trained, arrangements should have been made for regular giving and fund raising, and evangelistic work should have increased. In this way the church set its sights on the centenary, which was to be lavishly celebrated, with representatives invited from every corner of the Anglican Communion.

Janani gave unstinted thought and energy to the plan. He travelled hundreds of miles and spoke to thousands of people. He often illustrated his preaching with stories. To show the danger of selfishness, he would tell the crowds who flocked to hear him of the old man whose wife had died, leaving him with a baby boy. He took good care of the child. He never forgot to bring him food from the garden. But one day, he decided to put the boy to the test, to find out whether he would look after him in his old age. He gave the child some potatoes as usual but on this occasion asked the boy to share them with him. The child refused and hid the potatoes from his father. Yet the old man continued to care for the boy, until he grew into a man and married.

35

Janani explained: 'This is how we are with God. He gives us gifts, and when he asks us to give him back a little of what he gave us, so that he can use it to enlarge his kingdom and help the needy, we refuse. Yet still he continues to look after us, hoping that we will change and become good children.'

Janani's family were now eight in number, three boys and five girls. They wished he was at home more often. Many people wondered when Janani slept, since he was constantly either on safari or busy in the office preparing agendas and reports for what seemed like hundreds of committees which had suddenly mushroomed overnight. But Mary never grumbled and the girls were always ready with a flask of tea and a plate of roasted groundnuts.

Every ten years the bishops of the Anglican Communion gather for the Lambeth Conference. In 1968 all the Ugandan bishops went, and Janani went too, as one of the overseas consultants to the Archbishop of Canterbury. By now he was obviously a man marked out.

Janani's fellow tribesmen in Northern Uganda had followed his progress carefully and their hearts swelled with pride when they heard those in high places speak well of him. For a long time they had been pressing Archbishop Sabiti for their own diocese with their own bishop, but always the answer had been 'no'. So they were jubilant when news filtered through that the Archbishop, after returning from Lambeth, had at last agreed that the diocese of Northern Uganda should be divided. Janani was to be consecrated as Bishop of Northern Uganda; this diocese would now comprise Lango and Acholi. He was the first member of the Acholi tribe to become a bishop. Bishop Wani, already Bishop of the old diocese of Northern Uganda, would remain in his own district and be enthroned as Bishop of Madi and West Nile.

5. The People's Bishop

Janani's consecration took place on 25th January, 1969, in the large field known as Pece Stadium, in Gulu, the head-quarters of the new diocese. It was not just a religious ceremony, but a political rally. Dr Obote's government and the Church of Uganda were becoming increasingly linked together in people's minds. This was a natural conclusion, since the Uganda People's Congress was strongly Protestant, though Archbishop Sabiti resisted the temptation to accept an offer by the government to pay bishops' salaries.

Peter Abe, his former tutor, was given responsibility for all the local arrangements. A central committee was set up to organise the consecration, chaired by Janani's old friend and former headmaster of the school where he first taught, Erinayo Oryema (later to be murdered with him). They soon realised that the pro-cathedral of St Philip's Church was far too small to hold the large number of people likely to attend the consecration. Pece Stadium seemed the obvious place to stage the large open-air service.

The choice of Pece Stadium, however, was less obvious to Archbishop Sabiti and other church leaders in Kampala. They were horrified when the suggestion reached their ears. The stadium was used primarily for political rallies, football matches, athletic tournaments and Independence and Labour Day celebrations. Also they wondered if the members of the central committee had forgotten that the stadium was close to an area of dense private housing with a repu-tation for prostitution, the brewing of beer and harbouring of criminals. They were determined to stand firm about Pece but in the end they were overruled and forced to fall in line with the wishes of the political leaders in Kampala.

A week before the consecration, senior Acholi politicians from Kampala flew into Gulu to make certain all the plans were going well. There was much to do. An oval platform was built in the middle of the stadium, a huge red carpet was laid, flanked with artificial flower gardens, food was prepared for thousands of visitors, service sheets were printed and security was arranged for Archbishop Sabiti: an armed guard on duty all night.

There was only one unsolved problem: the heat and the dust of Gulu in January. This is the only month in Acholi when there is seldom a drop of rain, and the sun can be very hot. There seemed no solution. Peter Abe called together the members of his working committee for short prayers. That night, about nine o'clock, suddenly there was the sound of heavy rain. There was no wind at all. Peter felt even more upset. A really heavy downpour would destroy the beautiful work at Pece. All their efforts would have been in vain. But no – it rained for exactly one hour. God had worked wonders. Everything remained intact. Daybreak came and there was still no sun to be seen; the cloud sealed it off completely and was so thick that the weather remained cold, by Gulu standards, throughout the day. The dust raised by all the trucks that started to arrive was trapped by the rain of the previous night. The grass at Pece presented scenery that only the Almighty could arrange.

No one need have worried about the noise and the wrong sort of atmosphere in Pece Stadium. Police were stationed on all the roads leading into Gulu to warn lorry loads of people arriving late for the service that they must approach the stadium quietly; there would be plenty of time for merrymaking in the afternoon. So those in the stadium heard the noise of singing and drumming in the distance getting nearer and nearer and then suddenly stopping. During the consecration ceremony, Bishop Lyth of Kigezi preached about our Lord's first and last commands to Peter: 'Come with me' (Mark 1.17 NEB), and then, after all the joys and sorrows of those three years of companionship with him, 'Feed my sheep' (John 21.17). He addressed his words first to Janani: how he would come to the Lord with many problems and go out strengthened; come in penitence and go out forgiven. Many who were gathered at Pece that day took these words of Bishop Lyth to their hearts too.

Hardly anyone in Gulu had seen so many bishops together before. There were eleven present. The stadium was transformed with flowers and banana plants, and the altar was lifted on a high platform in the centre of the huge red carpet, so that everyone could see the minutest detail. The broadcasting system arranged by Radio Uganda was so good that everyone could hear. The police band accompanied the hymns. Thousands sang 'Lead us Heavenly Father, lead us', 'Now thank we all our God' and other lovely hymns in Lwo, the vernacular spoken by the Acholi and Langi, or in English, or in any language they knew.

Janani had asked for a 'special chorus' to be sung at his consecration. This turned out to be the Hallelujah Chorus from Handel's *Messiah*. Of the forty or so members of the choir, only Mr Aloya, the conductor, and Janet Lea, Bishop Wani's secretary, could read staff notation but everyone else had fluent tonic sol fa, and it was obvious from their very first practice that they could do it. On the day of the consecration, the Hallelujah Chorus almost took the choir off its feet.

President Obote and his wife were present with many ministers and other celebrities. The Catholic Archbishop, Emmanuel Nsubuga, was there. People's hearts burst in praise and thanksgiving. Many thought, 'How lucky we are in Uganda that we are able to worship in so much freedom and fellowship.'

After the service, Archbishop Sabiti led Janani to the edge of the red carpet where they were summoned to a halt by two children, a boy and a girl, carrying blossoms of *anyero*, special flowers given by the elders to those embarking on a dangerous journey. This was the signal the two hundred Bwola dancers had been waiting for. They began to sing:

Luwum	Luwum
Lam piny	Bless this land
Wek pacowa okwe	So that there is peace
Pi ber okelo	Our unworthiness
Kaca i Komwa	Shall finish us
Pi ber okelo	Our unworthiness
Ayela yee e i yee	Shall bring trouble
Eno Wod nyako	So son of a girl
Nen lawoko loko	Let live ones speak
Bako doge	Beseeching God

After his election Janani said : 'We feel it is a great honour and we are humbled because we know that the task facing the church in Northern Uganda is very challenging. None of us alone is sufficient for the task that lies ahead, but as we work together in God's strength we can have confidence for the future . . . ' He was well aware that the newly formed diocese of Northern Uganda was spiritually and financially poor with few committed leaders and his experiences at Lira Palwo confirmed in his own mind that the task confronting him was not an easy one.

The Anglican Church was weaker in Northern Uganda than in any other part of the country. A number of clergy had resigned. In many places church buildings had fallen down and no one had bothered to rebuild them. Congregations had dwindled and the giving was lower than it had ever been. A very bleak prospect indeed, for Janani. Yet almost immediately he arrived there was a sense of optimism. Janet Lea, who had now become his secretary, wrote in her diary a week after the consecration, 'With the Lord and Janani we will win.'

But Janani's first synod was stormy. The Acholi had put away their spears but they still relished hot debate, rivalry and quarrelling. The younger clergy and lay people were vociferous in demanding sweeping changes. The staff board met until midnight and decided nothing. Synod members harangued the bishop and one another. 'Everything must change with our new bishop,' was the cry. Janani begged members to give him more time to look and to listen before making decisions.

Committee meetings often continued until the early hours of the morning since every member was given a chance to speak. When I was secretary, the only way I found of stopping a meeting quickly was to fall asleep! In free moments between visitors or after office hours Janani would dictate answers to letters which came to him from many countries.

The giving in most parishes was meagre. Often the Church of Uganda pastors spent their time cultivating their *shambas*, or small gardens, in order to feed their families and failed to minister to their flock. 'Take the hoe out of your pastor's hands,' was one of Janani's messages in those early days in the diocese. 'I suddenly thought of those good words,' he told his secretary. 'Take the hoe out of your pastor's hands.

It seems to be getting across quite well.' But at the same time he offered words of comfort to the Christians at Christ Church in Gulu when their giving was slightly down at the end of the year. 'Never mind – you are building your vicar's house and that is a very good witness of caring.'

When Janani visited the parishes he tried to encourage the Christians to give from their hearts. A typical story he would tell was about a man who invited a friend to visit him. His friend accepted the invitation. A day was fixed for the visit, and his host invited other people to come and meet him. On the day of the party, everything was ready for the visitor. The home was clean. His host slaughtered a bull, goats and a chicken. It was a lovely day. The visitor arrived and was warmly welcomed. But when the food was served, the visitor was given only the head of a chicken to eat. He did not complain, but he knew his friend did not love him as much as he ought to do. Janani explained: 'We are like that unloving friend. We give God just a little. Yet we buy new clothes, meat and other things. Our hearts are far away from him. We love ourselves more than we love God.'

He was equally ready to tell a story against himself. On Rogation Day 1970, the vicar of Christ Church, Gulu, his curate and many lay people planned a service, during which a jar of water, a bowl of earth, seedlings and tools were taken into the sanctuary. The congregation thanked God for each of his gifts and offered themselves to his service. Janani addressed the large congregation: 'God has given us the rain and the sun and had given us Jesus,' he reminded them. 'What are you doing, all you influential people in this packed town church, to help our non-Christian friends?' He continued by relating how he had been driving home in the rain and dark with the archdeacon one night, when he had seen in his headlights a drunken man staggering about the road. 'I was hurrying to another meeting and I could foresee endless delays if I stopped and helped this man. I started to accelerate away. "Stop," said the archdeacon. "You cannot leave him there." ' He went on to tell how with a great deal of difficulty they had got the ragged, drunken man back to his home in the bush. This story made them realise how often they missed opportunities of showing Christ's compassion.

Janani revelled in his safaris to every parish in his diocese. He drove very fast. Maurice Lea, a CMS missionary almost old enough to be his father, rebuked him on one occasion. 'Bishop, will you please remember that you are very precious, and *drive more slowly*.' Janani merely responded with a schoolboy grin, half penitent and half proud of his achievement. He would argue that he had to drive fast in order to cover the vast distances between the parishes in the minimum time and to keep the car above the deep ruts caused by the top soil blowing away during the dry season. But there were often real hazards: bridges down, floods to negotiate, thick mud and a day or so later thick dust. The Catholic missionaries often found Janani stranded and had to dig or pull his car out of the mud.

Janani took a great interest in leprosy work in Acholi. At discharge ceremonies at the leprosy clinics, when patients would receive certificates that their leprosy was cured, he would take a short service of thanksgiving in Lwo. Once he asked a Catholic priest who was also present if he would like to take some prayers, but the priest replied, 'I am happy to say Amen. Prayer is the same for us all.' On another occasion a member of the local government administration, a pleasant young man, but never seen in church, from whom the visitors expected a political speech, said: 'People these days say there is no God, but how ridiculous when we can see things like fellowship between races and tribes, and people getting cured of their leprosy, none of which would happen if there wasn't a God.'

On one very splendid occasion Janani opened a sixteen-bed ward for leprosy patients near Gulu. This had been built with money from the West German Leprosy Relief Association and was the first new leprosy building in Acholi for many years. The service of thanksgiving had been planned jointly by Janani and the Catholic Bishop of Gulu, Cyprian Kihangire. The sun shone on the bougainvillaea; a breeze blew the gay striped curtains at the windows of the new ward; and the famous Acholi dancers moved gently through the vast crowd so that the bells on their legs did not disturb the speeches, as thousands of people waited to applaud, to sing and to dance. Janani gave thanks to God for the generosity of the people of West Germany and asked everyone to pray that Christ's love would shine like a light on all who came there for healing, of whatever tribe, race or religion.

He often quoted Archbishop Temple: 'My original sin is that I put myself in the centre of the picture. I don't belong there. God does.' It was difficult for Janani, loved and acclaimed by his people, to remain humble. Invariably the dancing and the presentation of gifts took longer than the service of worship.

There were failures too. The congregation at Christ Church, Gulu, planned with Janani to provide accommodation for girls newly arrived in the town. There was to be a coffee bar, a youth club and evening classes next door to the church; and a team of social workers, community workers and health visitors working in the low-income housing area of Pece.

At the same time Janani planned a Christian agricultural centre where members of village churches could receive training in Christian leadership and new farming methods. The old farm school in Gulu was standing idle, so he drew up plans to use it for this purpose, and he succeeded in getting funds from the German agency, Bread for the World, for both schemes. The agency allotted money amounting to two and a half million shillings.

Unfortunately no one could agree exactly how the money should be spent. The most popular suggestion, shared by Werner Reichart, the German development officer, and many of the Christians in the diocese, was that the farm school and the adjoining land should be developed commercially and the profits used to underwrite diocesan expenses, such as clergy salaries. Werner Reichart also wanted to use some of the money for loans to local farmers. Janani and others were not in favour of this, being afraid that the Christian aspect would be squeezed out. Janani also recognised the danger of the church becoming an employer, a potential exploiter of labour, which could alienate her from the very people she sought to help.

He sought a compromise that would include every shade of opinion. It was an attempt to reconcile the irreconcilable. At one meeting to discuss Werner Reichart's suggestion of a loan scheme, it was obvious that no one on the committee agreed with him. Janani allowed the debate to go on for six hours without reaching a decision. It seemed he was afraid

43

of offending the German benefactors. He never called another such meeting until the eve of his departure to Kampala in May 1974 after being elected Archbishop. Therefore no clear policies were ever laid down about how the money should be spent. Janani allowed Werner Reichart to go ahead and develop the two projects on his own initiative with only scant reference to himself and none at all to the other Christians. When Benoni Ogwal, Janani's successor, tried to rectify matters, he found that a large proportion of the money had been wasted. In the town the ambitious scheme never really came into being, except for two rooms which were erected in the grounds of Christ Church. The farm was never commercially viable. Most of the cattle died of tick fever. In the end the farm school buildings were refurbished as a diocesan training centre for church teachers.

There was failure then, as well as success, and always joy and sorrow in the diocese. Only a few days after a teachers' conference which had been marvellously happy, when Janani's sermon and the communion service he took had set the whole proceedings on the right path, he had to interview young men seeking an opening to go to Nairobi to train as a Church Army captain. Sadness overwhelmed him as the last candidate left the room. Only one or two of the applicants really knew the Lord, and most had come merely for the chance of a job.

Janani knew that the Church of Uganda would never take root unless its members were totally committed to Christ. There were few really committed leaders in the church in Northern Uganda and even those were often snatched by the central provincial administration. Janani would tell us: 'The harvest is plentiful, but the labourers are few' (Matt. 9.37). He often illustrated the need for commitment by telling the story of the hyena at the crossroads. First the animal would chase off down one road, then down another, but would never go far before returning to the crossroads again, fearful that there might be sweeter meat in the other direction.

And so a mission was planned for the diocese during April 1970. The theme was taken from Acts 26.18: ' . . . to open their eyes that they may return from darkness to light'. Janani told his diocesan staff that this meant not only a call to 'return' for the people who had lost their way but a heartfelt 'come' to all those who had never found it. Over a hundred missioners poured into Gulu from other dioceses. The meetings were rather sparsely attended at first, but as the week went on, the attendance improved. The climax was thrilling. After a packed and joyful Sunday morning service at Christ Church, a group of Christians set out together in a straggling but happy procession through the streets of Gulu, to Pece Stadium. Many hundreds of people marched with them. The Cross was lifted high as voices were raised in unison, 'Come to the Saviour, make no delay.' Janani ended the meeting with prayer that all those who had found new blessing would be given grace to stand fast and continue in the faith.

6. Amin's Coup d'État

Already, however, political disorder was threatening the good start that Janani had made as Bishop of Northern Uganda. On 20th December, 1969, news came through that Dr Obote had been shot at, and there was great unrest in Kampala. On 25th January, 1970, the first anniversary of Janani's consecration, there was a party in his garden by lamplight, to which many people had been invited. Next morning, the guests were to learn that at the time they had been happily celebrating, a group of armed men had shot General Amin's deputy, Brigadier Okoya, and his wife, only five miles from Gulu. There had been a rumour that President Obote had planned to appoint the brigadier as head of the army, replacing Amin, whom he strongly suspected had been behind the plan to assassinate him. The brigadier had also been an outspoken critic of Amin's personal bodyguard.

This murder was the beginning of a long line of political killings, which was to include Janani's own murder, and did not end there. Day after day Janani would come into the office for the afternoon's work looking sad and worried at something he had heard on the radio. Once he commented, 'The President is making powerful enemies.' For months Gulu was full of soldiers and rumours.

During the investigations that followed Brigadier Okoya's murder, the Ugandan CID built up a strong case against General Amin, maintaining that he was behind the brigadier's death. On the eve of his departure to Singapore to attend the Commonwealth Conference, Dr Obote issued a warrant for Amin's arrest. But he was not in time.

While it is true that there were people in Uganda who hoped for a *coup d'état*, the radio announcement on 25th January, 1971, that General Amin had seized control, took Uganda and the world by surprise. On the bishop's compound in Gulu people wandered between houses alternately listening to the radio and praying. At first it all seemed unreal.

Extracts from Janet Lea's diary at that time underline the grim reality of the *coup*, at any rate for the people of Northern Uganda.

26th January None of us felt like doing anything. There are many letters waiting for the bishop. Rumours flying. Still fighting in Jinja and Entebbe, but apparently jubilant Baganda are crowding the streets, singing and praising God, proclaiming General Amin as their saviour.

27th January The bishop decided we had better get some work done. It is very difficult to plan for the future.

29th January Bishop Elinana woke me at seven o'clock to say soldiers were firing and people were running just below our houses. Both bishops' houses were full of frightened people. Promised a school teacher to fetch his wife from a Roman Catholic hospital five miles from Gulu. There were no people on the road. On the way back with his wife and a darling baby, we met two jeeps tearing up from the town. They stopped. Armed men rushed to surround a house by the side of the road. Later saw all the offices shut. Accompanied Janani to town. We saw a body in the back of an army vehicle. District Commissioner's explanation – the man had been shot as an army deserter. Janani asked permission of the officer in charge of the police for me to visit the airstrip to collect my husband Maurice who was flying in from Entebbe. Permission granted. Accompanied by Festo, the bishop's chaplain. All along the road out of Gulu were hundreds of people with bundles on their heads, fleeing into the bush. Many children were lost – some drowned in the swamps in the panic that ensued. Drove really fast coming back to beat the curfew. People in small groups along the road, gazing in astonishment at a car going *towards* Gulu. Very scared. Shooting again in the night. We met an African friend who hadn't seen Festo for some time. 'How are you, Festo?' 'Only broken hearted,' he replied. But in

Kampala, we heard the Baganda were still dancing in the streets.

30th January We heard that 2,000 Acholi soldiers had been killed.

At Limuru, Kenya, in March, Janani and the General Secretary of the World Council of Churches, Philip Potter, were together for a meeting of the Anglican Consultative Council. They went for a long walk, during which Janani told Philip Potter of the terrible things that were happening in Uganda. He had no illusions about what was going on.

At the end of March, the *kabaka*'s body was flown home from England, where he had died. He was buried with full military honours. The Acholi fled into the bush, terrified that the Baganda would kill them when they saw their dead king. Janani also succumbed to his wife's pleading and with his family left Gulu to spend the days of the *kabaka*'s funeral at their home in Mucwini.

Following Amin's *coup*, a dark shadow hung over the Diocese of Northern Uganda. The suffering was intense. The Acholi and Langi were Amin's special target. Houses in Gulu were looted and many burned to the ground in their first purges. Military personnel were given extraordinary powers of arrest and instant execution.

Army vehicles full of soldiers roared through the country-side; going from village to village, they dragged out supporters of the deposed President Obote, threw them into prison, or shot them on the spot if they resisted arrest. Their bodies were thrown over the Kabalega Bridge into the river Nile or left on the roadside. Those found wearing shirts portraying Obote's head were forced at gun-point to eat them. A man accused of theft was tied to the ground by ropes in the centre of Pece Stadium in full view of a crowd who were forced to watch while soldiers on motor bicycles rode over him until he was dead. Deserters from the army were shot publicly in the market place. Those soldiers who obeyed Amin's call to return to their barracks were bayoneted and thrown into the river Nile. At Malire barracks, thirty-two senior Langi and Acholi soldiers were herded into a room and blown up by explosives. Langi and Acholi in the lower ranks were rounded up and crammed into the already crowded cells at Makindye prison.

Yet in many other parts of Uganda, the people were excited and optimistic. General Amin released political prisoners, including five former Obote cabinet ministers, and promised to hold free elections as soon as possible with all parties participating – including Obote's party. In fact, however, parliament was suppressed within a week.

Amin at this time had many supporters. He even gained credit for having tried to make peace within the Church of Uganda, where the rift had deepened to the extent of the Baganda calling Archbishop Sabiti a traitor, refusing him entry into Namirembe Cathedral and threatening secession from the province. They were sure that General Amin would restore the kingdom of Buganda, which Obote had abolished, and that he would put the *kabaka*'s son on the throne.

It was this rift between the Baganda and the rest of the Church of Uganda that Amin now attempted to put right. He surprised church leaders when he summoned all the bishops and diocesan councillors of the Church of Uganda to a meeting in Kampala in October, following an earlier gathering in Kigezi. He had heard that one diocese was threatening to secede, he said. He wished them to straighten out their affairs.

Bishop Festo Kivengere, in *I Love Idi Amin*, recalls the meeting:

For two days we sat and looked at one another, and differences remained. But on 28th November, the Lord gave us a message from Philippians. We saw that we were men going up, each one thinking about his reputation and demanding his rights. But that day, we caught a vision of the Man-coming-down: Jesus, 'Who, being in the form of God . . . made himself of no reputation, and took upon him the form of a servant, and was made in the likeness of men: And . . . he humbled himself even (to) the death of the cross.' What a change he made! In the presence of him who came down, our dear archbishop, Erica Sabiti, and each of the nine diocesan bishops, went down in confession of the sins which had contributed to the divisions in the church, and a great melting by the Holy Spirit came upon us all. President Amin has always, since then, laughingly reminded us that 'he saved the

Church!' But we know that Jesus, the One-coming-down, did it.

Janani continued his safaris to every part of the diocese but now he was greeted everywhere with the traditional wailing of the Langi and Acholi mourning their dead. He comforted those who mourned, encouraged the faint-hearted and urged us all to forgive as Christ forgave his enemies when he hung upon the Cross. He offered material help when he could, but wished the church had more funds to distribute to the growing number of widows and orphans.

He was fearful that a successful counter *coup* might carry in its wake more bloodshed as Acholi and Langi tribesmen sought revenge. He was well aware that the Acholi considered themselves an angry people who never apologise, pass judgement on their enemies, and never forgive. His continual plea, 'forgive your enemies, love those who persecute you,' fell on deaf ears. People brooded darkly.

It seemed at the time that the world closed its eyes and ears to the massacre of Acholi and Langi throughout 1971 and during the early months of 1972. Janani appealed to his brother bishops and after some hesitation they sought an audience with the President. Amin was both plausible and persuasive. 'The enemy has to be rooted out,' he insisted.

He began to acquire large quantities of arms. When Britain and Israel refused his requests, he turned for help to the predominantly Arab states and through President Gadaffi of Libya made extravagant purchases of military equipment, which soon strained Uganda's economy. He also sought to replace the Acholi and Langi soldiers by recruiting mercenaries from among those undisciplined Anyanya guerrillas from the Sudan who were considered unfit for work following the peace settlement which had ended the fighting in their own country.

The expected attempt at a counter *coup* came in mid-September 1972. Ugandan guerrilla forces invaded the country from Tanzania and soon newspapers were showing horrific pictures of the wounded and dead at Mbarara. But the invasion was badly organised and its failure was complete. Soon Uganda Radio was reporting that everything was under control. The soothing, over-persuasive voice of the news reader lulled people into a state of false security. Chaos reigned from September to December 1972. There were further purges of Acholi and Langi soldiers and civilians, but this time the killings were more widespread. A black list of civilians all over the country was drawn up. All the county chiefs of Ankole, where the invasion took place, were murdered. The Chief Justice, Benedicto Kiwanuka, a Mugandan, was killed for calling for a curb on the army's powers of arrest. He was dragged from the high court and dismembered alive. The vice-chancellor of Makerere University in Kampala was arrested and later executed in Makindye military prison. Their bodies, like those of thousands of others killed in similar circumstances, were never recovered. Official stories were circulated that they had fled the country.

This conflict was preceded by conflict within. The world had been unconcerned when President Amin expelled the Israeli community, whose technical advice had helped him organise the *coup*, because they refused to sell him arms. But when on 9th August he announced his intention of expelling from Uganda all Asians, both Pakistanis and Indians, who held British passports, there was a world outcry about the inhumanity and abruptness of the decree. There were over 50,000 of them and they had to leave within ninety days. Later the decree was expanded and applied also to 'any other person who was of Indian, Pakistani or Bangladesh origin, extraction or descent'.

After the announcement there was a frenzy of excitement in Uganda. Many Ugandans were pleased that the Asians were being expelled since they controlled certain areas of trade and commerce, and held many civil service posts and skilled jobs. Only a few were afraid of the damage to the economy that the sudden exodus of many rich merchants would bring. Departing Asians were intimidated at road blocks, their goods confiscated. Others burned their possessions openly in the streets. But at least the majority got away with their lives.

Janani had been attending the World Council of Churches' meeting at Utrecht in August when the news of Amin's decision to expel the Asians came through. It was a clear violation of civil rights and human liberties, but at that time it was difficult to get anyone to say out loud that any black man could do anything wicked. But at Utrecht an

Indian, a black American and a Nigerian brought forward a fairly strong resolution to be addressed to the Ugandan Government. Janani agreed to be one of a small group of four who met privately to draft the resolution which was finally passed. The text read:

> The Central Committee of the World Council of Churches, meeting in Utrecht, the Netherlands, expresses its deep concern over the disturbing situation reflected in the news about Uganda. While we do not presume to pre-judge the intention of the Government of Uganda with reference to its internal policies, we call upon the Government of Uganda to refrain from any actions which impair or deny the citizenship of Ugandans of Asian origin. Furthermore, we share a deep concern for other nation-alities in Uganda who are being affected by Government decree and other reported pronouncements.

Since the minutes of the Central Committee are eventually published and the whole session was open to the press, Janani must have known that the security forces in Uganda would be well aware that he had taken part in drafting such a criticism from an international body.

In Uganda everyone in the diocese longed for his return, though some were fearful for his safety. His outspokenness, his courage and his willingness to help all in trouble placed him in great danger.

I can still see him in my mind's eye – walking across the compound. It was the tenth anniversary of Uganda's Inde-pendence, 9th October, 1972. He flopped into a large chair on my veranda, buried his face in his hands and wept.

By Christmas that year everyone relaxed, buoyed up by the President's announcement that the country had returned to normal. Christmas in Uganda is always a time of feast-ing. There was still plenty of meat, sugar and salt. The road blocks had disappeared with the last plane load of Asians. 'We have won the economic war,' Amin declared with gusto and proceeded to allocate most of the businesses to mem-bers of his own tribe, army personnel, their relatives and friends, many of them brought in from outside Uganda.

In 1973 a new political pattern emerged. Periods of peace were followed, often abruptly, by fresh disaster. In February of that year, without warning, the President announced over the radio that a number of men had been arrested for subversive activities. The military tribunal ordered public executions in different parts of the country; each man was shot in his home community as a warning to others. Three men were shot in Pece Stadium, Gulu. They were young men, carelessly picked from the streets, their only crime being that they were in the wrong place at the wrong time. Pastors were allowed to visit the condemned men in prison. Many who were shot that day, in the different centres all over Uganda, repented and accepted Christ as their Saviour before they died.

On Maundy Thursday, Janani's daughter Florence died in Mulago Hospital. She had been ill for almost a year, and over the months her body had slowly wasted away. During one of her father's visits she asked him when Easter was. 'I am looking forward to Easter this year,' she told him confidently, 'because I shall be with Jesus.' None of the family was with Florence when she died; it happened so quickly. Coming so soon after the public executions, her death symbolised Christ's own death and resurrection and served as a reminder that Uganda was being drawn together by a common bond of suffering.

Over and over again we saw evidence of the Holy Spirit working in the lives of young people in the diocese. At a youth conference, a young teacher from Lango threw out the question, 'Can Jesus satisfy young people today?' There was an overwhelming response. Almost the entire company stood up and confirmed publicly that Jesus did satisfy their needs. Many came to Christ for the first time, others rededicated themselves, confessing that they had fallen away from the truth of God's word. During a service of worship the following morning, the Archdeacon of Gulu told his congregation that the previous evening, as he had approached the church to prepare for Sunday, his heart full of bitterness because his son had been murdered by the security forces, he heard the young people singing. 'A great peace flooded my heart. I want you to praise the Lord with me for his goodness and mercy. The Lord also spoke to me. In the past I had been critical of what I called "emotional evangelism". But the Lord challenged me to help these new converts to grow in the faith.' At the time it seemed that the Lord was recruiting for himself a mighty army to combat the evil which was beginning to take root in Uganda.

Janani preached regularly from John 8.31–2 : 'If you continue in my word, you are truly my disciples, and you will know the truth and the truth will set you free.' We prayed hard that the Lord would give us his strength and determination to continue and remain steadfast. I thought of the exiled Bishop Elinana's words before he returned to the Sudan. 'What happened in the Sudan,' he told us, referring to the civil war, 'will happen in Uganda one day. Use your time well to prepare the hearts and minds of the young people for the testing days ahead.'

The emphasis on calling people back to God was evident in other dioceses also. In October 1973, a group of us took part in the Soroti mission. I shall never forget going round with Janani and Ajaliah, an Acholi Christian, talking to assembled groups of people sitting beneath mango trees. I listened spellbound every day for a week as Janani spoke from Isaiah 1.18 : 'Come now let us reason together, says the Lord . . . though your sins are like scarlet, they shall be as white as snow; though they are red like crimson, they shall become like wool . . .'

These verses more than others speak of Janani's concern for his people, in his own diocese and in Uganda as a whole. He saw the faces of men and women, boys and girls – in the village, the office, the factory, the lavish homes on Tank Hill in Kampala, the army barracks at Malire . . . many estranged from God and from each other. He painted the picture of a loving Father weeping over his lost children whom he had cared for and tenderly brought up, and asking : 'Where are all my children, the beautiful girls, the handsome young men – where are they? Why have they left me alone? Even animals have more sense, the dog knows its owner.' His talks always concluded with a call to repentance, emphasising the need for us to say sorry to one another and to God, our Father; to put things right.

'Come now let us reason together, says the Lord,' was one of his favourite texts. He frequently used stories from the Old Testament, especially the ones illustrating forgiveness. 'Did you know that Jacob said sorry seven times when he came before Esau?' Eyes widened, boys nudged each other. 'Seven times' was caught and repeated in unison. His words were simple, direct; always challenging, they evoked response.

Janani continued to tour his diocese with unflagging energy. On his visits to parishes people would often ask him to come and sit in their homes and wait until everyone had arrived. 'Certainly not, we have come to work, not sit,' was always his reply. At one diocesan staff meeting, he spoke on the words from the Prophet Haggai: 'Work for I am with you, says the Lord of Hosts . . . My Spirit abides among you . . . fear not' (Hag. 2.4).

But the early days of optimism in the diocese had faded. Overshadowed by the *coup* and the intense suffering and depression that had followed, many people were bitter and fearful of the future. They found it hard to work and hard to forgive.

7. Archbishop and Leader

Archbishop Erica Sabiti, a man who walked closely with his Lord and Master Jesus Christ, guided the Church of Uganda through the turbulent years 1965–74. His own life had been transformed as a young pastor when the flame of revival had swept through Ankole in southern Uganda. Now frail in body, though not in spirit, dogged by recurrent illness, he pondered deeply over the question of his retirement. He knew he was not indispensable. But his position was not an easy one. He was afraid for his successor and the possible division over his selection. Prayerfully Erica Sabiti sought the Lord's guidance and it was just before the provincial assembly in August 1973 that he felt that the Lord had given him the green light. Accordingly he announced his intention to retire in May the following year.

Immediately people began to speculate and ask openly, 'Who do *you* think will be the next archbishop?' In the months that followed the name of Janani Luwum was often on people's lips. People liked what they saw. Janani was a good administrator, methodical and conscientious. They remembered with gratitude how at heated meetings the participants would refuse to start unless Janani took the chair, because he was known for his scrupulous fairness and desire to reconcile. He never took sides. This was his strength and his weakness. His opening words at every meeting he chaired were invariably, 'Gentlemen, let us bring everything into the light; let us throw down our weapons of resentment and pride and be open with each other.' If the discussion became very heated, he would say, 'Now friends, let us stand and just bring it before the Lord.' He was everyone's friend, young and old alike. No one was afraid to come to his office, to his home, to ask his advice, to share a problem or simply to talk and drink tea. The warmth of his greeting touched people's hearts and made them feel immediately at ease. They recognised his boldness and courage. He was never afraid to seek an audience with the President, if necessary alone, to share with him openly his anxiety about his own people, the Langi and Acholi, and others who had been arrested, detained or killed without trial.

But some of the *balokole* were doubtful about his spiritual qualifications. For in the diocese of Northern Uganda the flame of revival had petered out. A group of men and women whose hearts had been touched when the revival was at its height had broken away from the original *balokole* movement under their leader Yusto Otunno. Unlike the 'quiet *balokole*', this group were never content to act as leaven. Tramping from village to village, they became known as the 'trumpeters' or the 'noisy ones', since they proclaimed their message of repentance through megaphones. Even today, they gather in groups outside churches while a service is in progress. Their technique is a simple one. As soon as the last line of the final hymn dies away and the people begin to stream out into the hot sunshine, the shouting begins – words of repentance intermingled with words of abuse. While no one doubts their dedication and their sincerity, their noisy and often abusive words have caused friction in the church and division among the *balokole* in Northern Uganda.

Because Janani's name and Yusto Otunno's had always been linked together, some of the brethren in the south were cautious. They wondered about this man from Northern Uganda, where church attendance was poor, the giving meagre, church buildings almost non-existent and where the 'trumpeters' had smeared the name of the brethren. And although they recognised Janani's deep commitment to Christ and his mission, his preaching puzzled them. He always painted a gentle picture of God as a loving Father who waited patiently for his children to repent of their sins and return to him. 'Why are you wandering in the bush?' he would quietly ask the people. 'The Lord is saying to each one of you – "Repent – come home." ' As Janani's faith had matured over the years he had realised that it was better to love people into the Kingdom rather than frighten them. And they rarely heard him challenge people to make a public stand – to choose between life with Christ or death with the devil, a salient feature of most *balokole* meetings. Unfortunately some of the brethren tend to equate Christianity with repetitive evangelical testimonies and insist on the necessity of dramatic conversions. These were the ones who questioned the validity of Janani's own salvation. Perhaps they had forgotten, or maybe they had never known, since Janani tended to keep his experiences to himself, that he was one of the *balokole*.

As the date for the election of the new archbishop drew nearer, other names were mentioned and discussed openly. On 7th May, 1974, the bishops met at Namirembe to elect a new leader from amongst themselves. They voted twice. Each time Janani had the most votes.

Any doubts about Janani's spiritual qualifications finally evaporated when he publicly declared at Namugongo in June, at a service to mark the anniversary of the Ugandan martyrs, that he was in fact 'born again', using words familiar to the *balokole*. 'Many people,' he said, 'have learned about Christ as an academic exercise. The church must help such people to transfer Christ from their heads into their hearts. I had Christ in my head and not my heart before I was converted. In 1948 I was "born again" and Christ became the controller of my life. My sense of direction and values changed. Even now I am still growing in him.'

Janani's heart was heavy after his election. He was conscious that he was leaving his young successor, Benoni Ogwal, with many problems. There were divisions amongst the *balokole*; rivalry between the Church of Uganda and the Catholics. It is true that Janani himself enjoyed a good relationship with his Catholic brother bishop in Gulu, Cyprian Kihangire. He was also a prominent member of the Uganda Joint Christian Council, formed in 1964, and confidently told Anglican friends that this made possible a marvellous relationship with the Catholics. But alas, these magnanimous sentiments of goodwill between the two leaders were often not shared at parish level by the Church of Uganda pastors and church teachers, nor by the Catholic missionaries, who in the north were mainly Verona Fathers.

The schools were one area of rivalry. After independence in 1962, the government took over the responsibility for education in Uganda. In a complete reorganisation of the education system, schools founded by the Church of Uganda were now often given to a Catholic headmaster and vice versa, so that Anglican and Catholic pupils mixed together. The children were still segregated, however, during the time allotted for religious education.

It is not easy for a child of eight to know instinctively to which group he belongs. Sometimes Church of Uganda children joined the group of Catholic children being prepared for baptism. Occasionally an over-zealous Verona Father baptised children of Church of Uganda parents. When this happened the parents and the pastor rose up in arms to accuse the priest of 'sheep stealing' and reported him to their bishop. Long enquiries ensued which damaged hitherto good relationships and left bad feeling.

There was rivalry and division, too, over buildings. Parishes in Northern Uganda are large and the population is scattered over vast areas of bush. People walk miles to pray. Certainly there was more money available in the Catholic Church to finance the erection of church buildings. But the ideal site often seemed to be within striking distance of a Church of Uganda foundation school. The wrangling which frequently followed over the ownership of the piece of land often halted any further growth of either church, caused friction and impaired any good relationships which might have existed.

At Easter 1974, Sister Claudia, a nun of the Verona Order, was so scandalised by the division at the parish level between Catholics and Anglicans that she went to her bishop, Cyprian Kihangire, and told him that if Christians could not pray together at Easter, they might as well give up. She then went and told Janani the same thing. Both bishops responded to her challenge. They arranged a joint service for Maundy Thursday. Many were there to pray for unity. Chapter 17 of St John's Gospel was read, and this proved to be the beginning of joint Bible study.

This joint action, however, received a setback on the eve of Janani's departure to Kampala after his election as Archbishop. In a letter to Cyprian Kihangire, Janani rebuked by name a Catholic priest who was proceeding with his plans to erect a permanent church within a stone's throw of the Church of Uganda foundation school in the area, in spite of Janani's pleas that there should be discussion first. A group of Verona Fathers boycotted Janani's farewell. Sister Claudia was in tears.

There were other problems too, including general scepticism about religious belief and practice, according to both Christian and traditional principles. In African society, cause and effect is understood at two levels : first, how something happened, and second, why it happened at all. The first explanation is material, but the second and more important explanation is spiritual. In a time of disaster, such as the massacre of Acholi and Langi tribesmen after Amin's coup, one would expect a resurgence of religious interest with a return to the church, as was happening in other dioceses, or to the *ajwagi*, the traditional Acholi religious experts, as people sought an explanation for their suffering. Yet in northern Uganda this did not happen, even though this was the area worst hit by government terrorism. The Acholi are pragmatists and strongly materialist in their explanations. Why, they asked, should one look for a spiritual cause for their suffering when it is obvious that the record of Amin and his clique showed they would stop at nothing to get what they wanted? Amin, not God or the ancestors, was the cause.

The Lord called Janani to leave Northern Uganda without seeing any obvious fruits of the labours he put in. Once again his departure seemed premature. He longed for more time. But his spirits rose when he remembered the young people who sang and praised the Lord on Sunday mornings before they left to teach the children at Christ Church; the young man who had been accepted by the Church Army and had begun his course in Nairobi; and the young people who were beginning to join hands with their pastors and work with them when they returned home to the village.

The people rejoiced for Janani. They were proud of his achievement − his call to high office. They saw him as a paramount chief, not a 'servant of servants'.

But for Janani his departure was not a happy one. The letter signed by a group of Verona Fathers who had boycotted his farewell had cast a shadow over the occasion. He sat in the back of the car and allowed his driver to take the wheel, something he had never done before. As he drove away into the night, it was hard to believe that from now on he belonged to the Provincial administration. In the last few years we had grown possessive, even selfish. We had claimed him as *our* bishop, and had thought that Janani belonged to us.

On 9th June, he was installed as Archbishop in Namirembe Cathedral. Unlike the ceremony when he became a bishop, this was a simple service arranged by the church leaders themselves. President Amin did not attend. The crowd overflowed the building and those outside strained to hear what was going on. The ladies looked magnificent in their *basutis*. But in the midst of all this beauty and splendour there was a note of warning. Archbishop Olang' of Kenya related the story in Samuel of Saul and Agag, the king of the Amalekites. Saul knew that Agag was unclean. He belonged to another god. God commanded him to kill Agag but Saul spared his life. This was not an act of mercy but disobedience on Saul's part. Archbishop Olang' used this story as a parable to illustrate his point that God commands us to fight against evil. Many of us were challenged by his words because we knew that many evil practices were beginning to take root in Uganda at that time.

As a result of massive arms spending, Uganda's economy had declined rapidly since the expulsion of the Asians in 1972. Essential commodities such as building materials, cement, spare parts, margarine, toilet soap, sugar, salt, toothpaste, washing powder, stationery, torch batteries – even the simplest goods which had hitherto been produced in Uganda had to be imported, and as often as not they were smuggled over the border from neighbouring Kenya. Prices rocketed. Old women were pressed into remembering long forgotten recipes for making salt and soap. Ugandans struggled to get rich as quickly as possible at the expense of their poorer brothers. People hoarded the little they possessed, cultivated fields deeper and deeper into the bush, and allowed their houses on the roadside to collapse to stop soldiers plundering their granary stores. Many essential services, buses, taxis were beginning to break down. Factories came to a halt because spare parts and skilled technicians were scarce.

Janani warned against selfishness. One of his stories was about a man who had no food. God knew this, so he gave

61

him a portion of millet flour every day. This was enough for him, until the occasion when the man had a visitor. God realised he would require extra flour that day, so he gave the man two portions of millet flour instead of one. The visitor arrived, but his host said he had no food, and gave him nothing. 'Do not worry. These are bad days for us all,' replied the visitor. Evening came, and the man escorted his visitor home. On his way back he felt very happy. He was looking forward to eating the extra portion of millet bread. But when he asked his wife to prepare it, she found that both portions had been consumed by termites, and that day he also went without food.

As Archbishop, Janani was ready to co-operate with all the non-Christian and political groups within Uganda. He also sought to develop a close working relationship with the Catholic Archbishop, Emmanuel Nsubuga, the leaders of the different *balokole* groups, and Stephen Mungoma, the leader of the Deliverance Church, a recently formed charismatic group. He asked to share a room with Mungoma at Lausanne during the International Congress on World Evangelism in order to draw alongside the young man and understand his aspirations more deeply.

The Church of Uganda felt threatened by the work of the Deliverance Church and other pentecostal groups who had discovered a new life in the power of the Holy Spirit. Many church members were quick to criticise and condemn and they urged Janani to take a strong line and drive out the members of the Deliverance Church. But he would reply: 'Those brethren of the Deliverance Church are doing a good job in bringing men to Christ. It is because they assume that we have not had a "charismatic" experience that they tend to cause division. We are a young church and need the support of all Christians.'

His respect for Christians irrespective of their beliefs kept many within the Anglican family when they felt other Christians misunderstood their point of view and uttered unkind words. But his ready desire to reconcile by finding a compromise could be a fault. Once, in Northern Uganda, two members of a Board arranging certain projects, speaking in all Christian love and fellowship, had strongly argued their respective cases for and against a particular course of action, when Janani summed up by saying that he felt sure we all agreed with both speakers! He had sensed division and as always sought to reconcile the sometimes irreconcilable. Amid laughter, the matter was resolved amicably.

At this time Janani was still communicating freely with the President. It was not unusual in those early days for Amin to telephone him in the middle of the night to ask his opinion on state matters. The two men would speak in Lwo, one of the Nilotic vernaculars. Sometimes the presidential car would arrive unexpectedly at the provincial offices with a message that the President wished to see the Archbishop immediately.

Janani quickly established himself in the office. Mary, however, did not slip so easily into Kampala life. She hated the limelight and would have preferred to remain in the background as in Northern Uganda she had been able to do. Mary was happiest with a baby on her back, cultivating their fields in Mucwini. But she put her feelings on one side and accompanied her husband to the innumerable government receptions and on his safaris to every part of the Province.

He was an immediate success. Wherever he went – to neighbouring countries such as Zaire, Rwanda or Burundi, or to widely differing areas of Uganda – he was greeted by jubilant crowds. Lavishly entertained, showered with gifts, he loved it. 'They are very wild up here,' he would say, referring to the entertainment, but by the broad grin on his face I knew he was enjoying every moment of the gay spectacle of swirling skirts and wild drumming.

A safari with him and his entourage was rarely without incident. Once the Christians from Mucwini, his home village, asked him to lay the foundation stone of their new church. The walls were complete but there was no roof. Many people had gathered in the new building and were waiting patiently for the Archbishop's procession to arrive. The sun beat down unmercifully. They waited and waited. Eventually Mary Luwum got up and with one accord the whole congregation followed her and settled down thankfully beneath the trees. A few minutes later the Archbishop's procession arrived and found the church completely empty.

One safari that took him over the border to neighbouring Zaire, to the part known as Boga, is typical of many. The original plan was to leave Kampala at seven in the morning.

At noon he was still in the office. Eventually they left, only to discover after many miles that the Archbishop's robes had been left behind. His secretary, Sylvia, telephoned from a trading post, asking for the robes to be brought. At four thirty in the afternoon they were still waiting. It was ten o'clock before they reached the border, very tired and hungry, and that night they had to sleep rough. At the border, Sylvia, the only white person in the party, was suspected of being a spy. 'She is a mere child,' protested Janani, concealing a large grin.

The roads were dreadful, pitted with huge potholes. In some places the surface almost petered out. On the way to Boga, their destination, it rained and rained. At one point they were completely stuck in the mud. They all got out and pushed and eventually, much to everyone's relief, got on to firmer ground. Boga, shown on the map as a town, consists really of a mere handful of family settlements and a few small shops. But it is a powerful Christian centre. This is the place from which the small Anglican Church in Zaire grew, after the evangelist Apolo Kivebulaya brought the gospel there from Uganda at the turn of the century. In this part of Zaire there are hardly any roads. The Archbishop's party trekked through the bush day after day. Along winding paths they walked, in single file, across stream beds, through tall forests. Their feet got wetter and wetter. When they came to the flooded river, off came their shoes, and they waded through water thigh deep with trousers rolled up above the knees and long skirts hitched up. Sylvia was amused by the incident. 'Have you ever seen an Archbishop and two bishops with coats over their arms, purple shirts and silver crosses dangling, wading through water up to their knees?' she asked after her return.

The time when the state authorities of Uganda had looked with favour on the Church of Uganda was over. For President Amin comes from the only predominantly Muslim tribe in Uganda – the Kakwa, situated on the borders of the Sudan, Uganda and Zaire. Many of them are Nubians who have been known as ruthless fighters ever since they were brought into Uganda at the turn of the last century as mercenaries by Lord Lugard. Amin identifies with any who say that 'the gun is their mother, father, and brother.' It is from the Nubian community, who are almost exclusively Muslim, that Amin has drawn all his top advisers since his accession to power. The Nubians never integrated with Ugandans; they lived in their own exclusive communities in urban areas. Unfortunately the church failed to recognise the importance of taking the good news of Christ's death and resurrection to them while the door was still open, and now it is closed and barred.

President Amin's aims became clearer as Christians who held administrative posts in the government were removed and Muslims took their places. An increasing number of ministries were headed by high ranking Nubian Muslim army officers. The government ruthlessly took over businesses owned by Christians and distributed them to army families and Nubians.

Increasingly Amin looked towards the Islamic states for help. He won their support by his continual abuse of the Israeli government on the radio. President Gaddafi is reported to have told Amin, 'You are a prophet! As I see you, I see another Muhammad. Be brave, and we will support you!' King Faisal of Saudi Arabia also visited Uganda. He gave President Amin royal gifts – an enormous platter of gold and a golden sword. He told him, 'With this sword make your country Muslim.' More and more of Uganda's now limited produce was flown to the Arab States. On a journey from Gulu to Kampala we passed a group of lorries crammed with cattle. 'More cows for Libya,' remarked Janani. Later we passed a second group of lorries, again full of cows. 'More cows for Libya,' we said. Janani replied: 'Never mind, the Lord is sending us food from heaven.' He had just swerved on to the side of the road and killed two guinea fowl.

And so Muslims began to dominate this predominantly Christian country. At the last British census, Muslims were shown to make up only about six per cent of the population. Misled by Amin's assurances, President Gaddafi accused the British of having falsified the statistics. At Makerere University in Kampala many students walked out during President Gaddafi's visit to the university when he told them that Libya was giving Uganda money to 'eliminate the few remaining Christians and turn Uganda into a Muslim state'. After his visit, the head of the Department of Religious Studies at Makerere at the time, Professor John Mbiti, spoke against the Muslim tactics when he declared in a sermon: 'Christianity and Africa have fallen in love with each other and intend to be united in the bonds of a life-long marriage. Christianity is here to stay.'

Just before the Organisation of African Unity met in Kampala in August 1975, Amin deported sixteen Catholic missionaries from northern Uganda while their Bishop, Cyprian Kihangire, was in Rome. Four Anglican missionaries were similarly dismissed. No consultation had taken place beforehand with the two churches nor were any adequate reasons given for this action.

Stringent regulations were introduced governing the movement of all Christian religious leaders and in a private letter President Amin accused Janani of helping government officials who had fallen from favour. Janani replied that in the Old Testament people on the run from the authorities would grasp a leg of the holy table. 'In the same way, our Christians run to me.'

It seemed that a web of evil was being spun and more and more people in Uganda were finding themselves caught in it. Family after family had one or more of its members accused by the security forces, arrested, beaten and often killed before investigations could be made or any trial held. Life had become cheap. Bodies were regularly found floating on Lake Victoria or caught amongst the papyrus, or buried carelessly in shallow graves. Others were burned in petrol fires or simply thrown into the bush and left there to rot or be eaten by wild beasts. There was a smell of death from the marshes. The crocodiles which basked contentedly on the banks of the River Nile were fat. One young girl whom I had not seen in church for some time told me she could no longer bring herself to go after she had tripped over a body in the road.

People whose faith had been shattered, their hopes smashed, sought refuge in Janani's office. A lady would come and say, 'I've not seen my husband for a week. I don't know where he is. I think he has been picked up by the army.' Janani would leap into his car and go in person to the offices of the dreaded State Research Bureau. If he drew a blank there, he would contact the officers in charge of the Public Safety Unit. Both these groups had been given power to arrest civilians, and most of the time they took the law into their own hands and executed their victims on sight. If people came quickly to see Janani, he might trace a husband or son. Occasionally he secured their release, but often he was too late. It was Janani who insisted that the British lecturer Denis Hills, a Catholic, should receive pastoral care while in prison.

Such was the background as during 1976 plans for the Church of Uganda's centenary the following year began to gather momentum. A full-time member of staff was appointed to co-ordinate all the centenary activities. People were bursting with ideas. Hundreds of people from overseas had been invited including the Archbishop of Canterbury, Dr Coggan, and a number of other bishops from the Anglican Communion. Two million centenary badges, thousands of T-shirts, caps and ties were on order. Every diocese was writing up its own history. The National Theatre had been approached and asked to stage a play portraying the story of the Ugandan martyrs. It was hoped that the climax of the centenary in Kampala would be declared a public holiday so that everyone would be free to attend the service of thanksgiving and rededication. Plans were also going ahead for the building of Church House, a multi-storey building, in Kampala's city centre, as a memorial of one hundred years of Christianity in Uganda. Evangelistic missions were planned in every diocese, conventions and a clergy conference, as well as all the special diocesan centenary activities.

At a meeting of the House of Bishops, Janani told his brother bishops, 'I do not want to be the Archbishop of a dead church, but of a live one.' He pictured our Lord Jesus Christ standing in the world of Palestine and looking north in front of him into the far distance, then west on his left hand and east on his right, and then behind him to the south. He saw the whole of Europe, Asia, Australia, Africa – unreached by the gospel. And he asked, 'How can we find so many mouths, so many hands, so many feet to take the gospel across the world?' Janani went on: 'Many men and women responded, "Lord, here am I – send me." This is how the gospel came to Uganda.'

Festo Kivengere, now Bishop of Kigezi, had reported on his visit to Britain with two other Ugandan evangelists in 1974. 'Britain is hungry for the gospel,' he told the bishops.

67

Janani responded: 'Brothers in the Lord, by the time our church celebrates its centenary, we must be ready to move out – to send missionaries overseas.'

But many of the centenary plans required the President's blessing, his stamp of approval on the Church of Uganda's application for foreign currency and a firm assurance that visitors' permits would be available. Janani almost reached desperation. His many letters to the President asking for an appointment to discuss the arrangements for the centenary were never acknowledged. The Mothers' Union also had their own centenary to celebrate – in London that very year, 1976. The Church of Uganda proposed to send over eighty delegates, but the President would not discuss this plan either. It was not until the beginning of March that he finally summoned Janani to meet him. The discussion was hurried and Amin gave only a few verbal assurances about the centenary. But he did agree to release an adequate sum of foreign currency to allow the Mothers' Union delegates to travel to London.

The way ahead looked clearer and there was general rejoicing in the Church of Uganda. Soon after the meeting with the President, in the middle of March, Janani travelled to the Caribbean to attend the meeting of the Anglican Consultative Council, the executive body of the Lambeth Conference. He went with a lighter heart. He was excited about the centenary and communicated his own enthusiasm and the excitement of the Church of Uganda as a whole, to the many church leaders, Christians and friends he met during brief visits to England, Canada, and the United States of America on his way back to Uganda in mid-April.

While he was in the Caribbean, Janani wrote to my bishop, Benoni Ogwal, in Northern Uganda asking him to release me to work in Kampala. I was reluctant to go. Gulu was my home and I felt secure amongst the Acholi. But of course I obeyed.

When I arrived the provincial office was humming with activity. The centenary co-ordinator's office looked like a warehouse. Loads of T-shirts and badges kept arriving and the overflow spilled into the corridor. Janani was bubbling with joy and excitement. Teams of missioners were beginning to go out from every diocese. News reached us of business men, young people and villagers committing their

lives to Christ in hundreds. At a big convention in Ruwenzori it was impossible to count the number of people who
came forward and humbly knelt before the altar which
had been erected on the hillside, for they stretched as far
as the eye could see. 'Perhaps we should not even try to
count them,' Bishop Rwakaikara whispered to Janani. In
Bunyoro thousands had come running to hear the word of
God preached during a week of evangelistic meetings. In
Kigezi, Bishop William Rukirande declared they were sending out teams of missioners all the time.

But there was also frustration and anxiety. In the office
we were alternately praising or weeping. We rejoiced when
the eighty Mothers' Union delegates held their final meeting
in Kampala, packed their cases and were ready to leave.
But we wept when news came through that the Church of
Uganda's application for foreign currency had been with-
drawn. Janani was out of the office at the time, on safari in
Northern Uganda. But he took the matter up immediately
with the President, pointing out that Uganda's image overseas would be badly damaged if no delegates arrived in
London for this international gathering. Finally, after much
persuasion, the President agreed with reluctance to allow
three delegates to fly to London at the end of May.

The Catholic Church was similarly disappointed when
their application was turned down for a group of Catholics
to accompany Archbishop Nsubuga to Rome for the ceremony of his installation as a Cardinal in St Peter's. Only
three people went with him. On his return, however,
jubilant crowds who had gathered at Entebbe Airport to
welcome him home pushed his car all the way to Kampala,
a distance of twenty miles.

The Cardinal and Janani were often together. They comforted each other. The Cardinal said he hoped things would
be better before the time came for the Catholics to celebrate
their own centenary in 1978.

8. Storm Clouds Gather

On Namirembe Hill we lived as a family and we discovered that love blots out fear as we drew closer to Christ and each other. Food was short and there was very little water. Kampala seemed a lonely place, a city full of rumours. No one ventured out after sunset and at night people lay awake fearful of a midnight knock on the door, while only the howl of dogs pierced the stillness.

A new martyr was made in Uganda in June that year when Teresa Nanziri-Bukenya, the warden of Africa Hall in Makerere University, was murdered. She had been recently married and was eight months pregnant. A Catholic, she was respected and loved by all the students. The authorities had tried to get her to sign a false statement about the disappearance of a Kenyan girl and she had refused. When he heard of her death Janani wept.

In July, terrorists hijacked a French plane on its way to Tel Aviv and forced it to land at Entebbe. As the 106 Israeli passengers were separated from the rest, it gradually became clear that the government of Uganda was acting in concert with the terrorists. Then came the dramatic landing at Entebbe of Israeli commandos and the rescue of all the hostages, followed by the anger and revenge of the Ugandan security forces. Soldiers roamed the streets during the days that followed, arresting and killing.

There was a new crisis over the murder of Dora Bloch, the British Jewess who had been receiving treatment in Mulago Hospital. Amin denied all knowledge of her whereabouts, telling the British government that she had been discharged by the doctors from Mulago and had rejoined the other passengers at Entebbe. In fact, she had been dragged out of her hospital bed and murdered.

In a tirade of abuse over Uganda Radio, President Amin accused President Kenyatta and his government of being Zionist supporters since they had allowed the Israeli planes to refuel at Nairobi airport on their way to Entebbe, and to set up a field hospital to care for the wounded on their return journey. In reply President Kenyatta reminded Amin of his trading debts to Kenya, and declared that until the accounts were settled he would allow no more lorries to cross the border. This action almost paralysed Uganda. Within a few days Kampala's petrol stations were drained dry as people scrambled to fill cans and other utensils. Racketeers sold petrol on the black market and to make it go further added water. People with cars, who had previously driven to work, walked or stayed at home. Public transport came to a halt. It was considered a privilege to ride on a government lorry, crammed in like cattle. Later, Amin's soldiers raided houses and shot those hoarding petrol. It was only army personnel who moved freely. Government and church officials and institutions were given a small allocation of petrol. Mengo Hospital in Kampala, for instance, was allowed to keep one ambulance on the road. Water pumps stopped. Young girls carried water from the streams, and each day we prayed that the Lord would bless us with rain. It was not until the end of August that petrol flowed back into Uganda, when the rift with Kenya was temporarily healed.

The British community now quietly withdrew from Uganda, except for a handful of missionaries and businessmen who decided to stay at their own risk.

Immediately after these events trouble broke out at Makerere when the students who returned in mid-July to begin their new academic year learned of Teresa Bukenya's murder. They were horrified, and wanted to stage an immediate strike to register their protest. The vice-chancellor forbade them to strike, pointing out that this would be misinterpreted and would be labelled as Zionist. Quietly indignant meetings were held in private rooms. Amin's son had recently joined the university to learn English. The students were uneasy. He regularly flourished his gun when he met them and threatened to shoot anyone who annoyed him.

It was late in the afternoon of Tuesday, 3rd August, when

71

we first heard that the army had surrounded Makerere. Janani immediately went to the university, but the offices were closed and there was no sign of the army. During the evening all kinds of rumours began circulating and the following morning Janani returned to the campus, this time with Cardinal Nsubuga. They went together to see the vice-chancellor, who agreed there had been trouble; some students had staged a strike, he said, but their demonstration meeting had been quickly quelled and lectures were proceeding as usual. Later that day, however, we heard a different story. A friend of one of the students who had gone to Makerere told us that the army had swept in, broken down doors, beaten students with their gun butts, made them crawl on hands and knees over gravel and through mud and repeat over and over again, 'We are fools, we are fools.' His friend had been one of the hundred students packed into army trucks and taken to the military prison at Makindye. They expected to be shot. But then the vice-president arrived at the prison and ordered the soldiers to stop beating them. They were given hot cups of tea, subjected to a long speech on patriotism and loyalty, and told to behave and attend their classes. It was perhaps Janani's prompt action in going straight to the campus when he heard the first rumours that saved the lives of these students.

But worse was to come. In the early hours of Wednesday morning the army returned. The second raid was more vicious than the first. Students were forced to jump from upper storey windows, others were raped. When the soldiers left, there were students with broken backs, fractured skulls, and serious wounds.

Neither the Catholic Church nor the Anglican Church in Uganda had any tradition of social or political criticism. But now they were forced to take up political positions.

Thieves, soldiers, mercenaries and police were all looting and killing at will in the name of the government. In July a Catholic priest had been taken away at gunpoint while he was celebrating Mass. Later his body was found a few miles away. There were also reports of growing animosity between Christians and Muslims. In one trading centre in West Buganda sacred books in the mosque had been burned. In Ankole in western Uganda fighting had broken out between

Muslims and Christians and as each group sought revenge they burned each other's villages. Many people had been arrested and others had disappeared.

At a general meeting to discuss the breakdown of law and order in Ankole, the Governor alleged that the religious organisations were to blame. They were using their places of worship, he said, to preach politics and to raise money to overthrow the government. His words disturbed the religious leaders who were present – the Catholic bishop, the Church of Uganda bishop, and the Muslim kadi – and they asked to meet him privately. Afterwards all three of them signed a joint letter exhorting their respective followers to work together in love and harmony, not to harass those of another religion, not to preach politics and to inform the government authorities when they intended to hold large meetings and raise money for special projects. This letter is a document of great ecumenical importance.

I believe it was the joint initiative of the religious leaders in Ankole that finally prompted Janani and Cardinal Nsubuga to take action. They agreed to call the bishops of both churches to a joint meeting at Lweza, the Church of Uganda conference centre, six miles from Kampala, and they invited the leader of the Muslim community – the Sheikh Mufti of Uganda – and Bishop Novoratis of the Uganda Orthodox Church to attend also. Only the Orthodox were unable to come, since Bishop Novoratis was out of Kampala at the time.

I drove to Lweza with Janani on the morning of Thursday, 26th August. Past the vanilla plantation we went, and up the winding drive to the large house overlooking the lake, which shimmered in the bright sunlight. Soon other bishops began to arrive. The warden, Elisha, and his wife served coffee. There were roasted groundnuts and bananas. The Muslims did not join the small intimate groups dotted here and there over the vast expanse of lawn sweeping down to the lake. They were fasting during Ramadan and waited patiently for the consultation to begin in one of the conference rooms.

The religious leaders gathered at Lweza convinced that it would be wrong to remain quiet any longer about what was happening in Uganda, but no agenda had been fixed and no chairman appointed. Janani was asked to chair the meeting.

73

I was one of the secretaries. They discussed the killings, the harassment, the looting, the excessive power given to the intelligence officers. In the minutes of their meeting they noted the shortage of essential commodities and the consequent rise of a black market. Their comments included the criticism that in some places people who were entrusted with the responsibility of ensuring fair distribution were 'themselves involved in corrupt practices'. As a result, they said, the common man suffered at the expense of the wealthy élite. They suggested a price list for all imports; and that religious leaders and government officials should work together to ensure that essential commodities were fairly distributed. They stressed the feeling of insecurity among the people of Uganda. The minutes stated that 'rumours were circulating in one area of a black list. Consequently people had begun to live in fear of their lives and properties. Mention must also be made of the many armed robberies resulting in serious injuries and sometimes death of the victim . . .'

Then the religious leaders examined the root cause of all these conflicts and evils in society. They attributed it to 'jealousy, personal animosity, paying back evil for evil'. They said that 'people found themselves accused by unknown persons, arrested, beaten and sometimes killed before proper investigations were made and a proper trial arranged. People were arrested by members of the State Research Bureau and the Public Safety Unit and not taken to a court where proper justice could be administered. Many of these people had disappeared.'

They suggested steps that should be taken. As the minutes recorded: 'Members felt that civilians should not be arrested by the military police. The military police had been set up to apprehend soldiers. Members suggested that civilians should only be arrested with a proper signed warrant by an officer of the civil police in uniform. The government should respect its own channels of communication and work in close collaboration with government officials and chiefs in the area.' A later paragraph added: 'Members asked that as religious leaders they should be informed before expatriate staff were deported and if possible given the reason for their deportation, to ensure that the same error was not repeated.'

They respectfully requested an interview with the President, to talk things over, to share their concern. Amin never granted their request. Instead, through his permanent secretary for religious affairs, he sent an angry reprimand to Janani for holding the meeting without permission. At the same time, he demanded the minutes of the meeting. They sent him their document in the usual way, properly signed by the chairman, Janani Luwum, and the secretaries of the three religious groups, including myself for the Church of Uganda.

From this time Janani was a marked man. At the Lweza meeting, the churches had emerged as a vocal opposing force. Janani was seen by the government authorities as their leader.

The preaching of both churches, Anglican and Catholic, now became more direct. 'Uganda is killing Uganda,' Janani told the men at the police barracks at Nsambya during an official visit at the end of August. 'We look to you to uphold the laws of our land. Do not abuse this privilege.' Afterwards some thanked him for speaking so openly, and showing them so clearly their responsibility. But others were afraid his words would annoy the President, whose anger might fall on them.

Janani continued to attend government functions. Once, loath to attend a reception Amin gave for British personnel working in Uganda, I shared my uneasiness with Janani. 'You must go,' he told me. 'Even the President needs friends.' He would say : 'We must love the President. We must pray for him. He is a child of God.' He feared no one but God who was the centre of his life. But his wish that the Church of Uganda should have a guiding influence upon the government misled some people, who complained that he lived a comfortable life and was on the government side. When the Archbishop met one of his critics in December, he made clear the truth. In words that proved prophetic, he told him: 'I do not know for how long I shall be occupying this chair. I live as though there will be no tomorrow. I face daily being picked up by the soldiers. While the opportunity is there, I preach the gospel with all my might, and my conscience is clear before God that I have not sided with the present government, which is utterly self-seeking. I have been threatened many times. Whenever I have the opportunity I have told the President the things the churches disapprove of. God is my witness.'

On Christmas Day Janani prayed for peace. He spoke of the social sins which destroy peace, such as an unforgiving spirit, jealousy, hatred and greed. His message on the radio was cut short. 'Some bishops are advocating bloodshed,' announced the President, and he personally threatened those who continued to speak what he called 'words of treason'. No one knew which church he meant. The Catholics thought the threat was directed at them, while the Church of Uganda concluded that he meant them.

The Christmas holiday was cut short and Boxing Day and New Year's Day were declared working days. Just before midnight on New Year's Eve, a group of us climbed Namirembe Hill and sat on the steps outside the cathedral. As drums in the distance heralded 1977, the centenary year of the Church of Uganda, we read Psalm 73. The words of David – 'I nearly gave up' echoed our feelings. Like him, we too had nearly lost confidence, our faith too was almost gone because we saw daily that things went well for the wicked.

The problems of Uganda were too difficult for us. As we sat on the steps together, we realised afresh, like David, that our only salvation was in renewed commitment to God. We prayed for Uganda, and for ourselves, that all of us would find a new reality in David's prayer: 'But as for me, how wonderful to be near God, to find protection with the Sovereign Lord and to proclaim all that he has done!' (Ps. 73.28 Living Bible).

9. The Martyrdom

Bushenyi is where the climax began: a lovely part of the country, rolling hills covered with banana plantations and cows. It was the last weekend in January. The diocese of Ankole, in the south, had been divided into two and Yorum Bamunoba was to be consecrated as first Bishop of West Ankole.

We left Kampala on the Friday morning, 28th January, Janani, Mary, and myself. George, his driver, was at the wheel – driving too fast at times, but we were anxious to arrive in time for lunch and to prepare for the bishops' meeting scheduled for the afternoon. There was an extraordinary feeling of excitement. Janani had consecrated and enthroned many bishops since his own installation in June 1974, so the consecration and enthronement of Yorum Bamunoba was routine, just another engagement in a very busy programme. Yet all roads led to Bushenyi that weekend. Everyone, it seemed, was planning to come. Hundreds had been officially invited: the government, the army and the Christians. The stage was set for a drama the world will never forget.

We arrived too early. The staff of the Farm Institute at Bushenyi had been firmly convinced that we would not be there before evening and were still relaxing, surrounded by notices they had painted to help people find the place. But when Janani was around no one remained idle for long. People were dispatched to fix the notices so that the other bishops would be able to find the place more easily, and there was a frantic squawking of chickens in the bushes. Shortly afterwards Bishop Amos Betungura arrived with his wife and while we waited for lunch we enjoyed cake and soda which nicely took the edge off our appetites. Lunch was served at four o'clock, the first of a succession of feasts.

Other bishops began to arrive and Janani announced that the first session of the House of Bishops would begin shortly after tea. The meeting was a leisurely affair because there were so many breaks for refreshment.

The service of consecration and enthronement was at Bweranyangi, the new diocesan centre on the neighbouring hill. Since the church building was small the Christians had arranged for the congregation to sit outside underneath a huge canopy of banana leaves. From early morning people began to arrive – on foot, on bicycles, in lorries and cars. The crowd grew to an estimated thirty thousand. A lady from Kampala, somewhat overwhelmed by the constant stream of people steadily climbing the hill, remarked, 'I expect they are coming for company. These days people have nothing to do to relieve the boredom.' I replied, 'I don't think so. They have come to hear the gospel.'

There was a determination that day that everyone was going to hear the gospel, even the security men hiding in the bushes. The three sets of microphones were so clear that you could hear every word half a mile away.

The preacher, Bishop Festo Kivengere, took his text from the Acts of the Apostles: 'But I do not account my life of any value nor as precious to myself, if only I may accomplish my course and the ministry which I received from the Lord Jesus, to testify to the gospel of the grace of God . . . Take heed to yourselves and to all the flock, in which the Holy Spirit has made you guardians, to feed the Church of the Lord which he obtained with his own blood . . . ' (Acts 20.24, 28).

His words are still ringing in my ears. 'Don't guard your own life . . . it is precious in so far as it is useful to preach the gospel. If you preach the truth, expect to meet the devil head on.' Then suddenly Bishop Festo was out of context. 'Remember, all authority comes from God. God uses his authority to uphold a man. How are you using your authority? To uphold or to trample, to crush men's faces into the dust? God is going to judge how each one of us here is using his or her authority. Judgement is not ours, it belongs to God . . . '

A show of power with a battery of words. God's name was upheld that day at Bweranyangi.

After the service there was a huge feast. They were well

78

prepared, the Christians of West Ankole. Twenty cows had been slaughtered, six hundred crates of soda had been delivered and the bunches of uncooked *matoke* stood as high as a tree. Everything at Bweranyangi was done on a grand scale. Even the new bishop's throne was the largest I had ever seen. It had been made locally and donated by one of the Christians.

In the evening as we drove back to Kampala we passed many cars full of security officers. I wondered what they would tell the President when he asked what it had been like at Bweranyangi and how many people had been there. The anniversary celebrations of the Second Republic the previous weekend, when most people had stayed at home, must have seemed like a damp squib in comparison. In Soroti they had been able to muster only fifty children for the march past and everyone had walked out when the drinks were served. I was unaware that George drove most of the way at nearly a hundred miles an hour since my one thought was to get home to communicate the challenge of Bweranyangi to others of our fellowship group which met on Sunday evenings. I was able to share Bishop Festo's sermon with them and as we prayed we asked the Lord to help us to testify to the truth of his word. We knew in our hearts that the Lord was preparing us for something big; he had told us over and over again, 'Don't fear death.' He asked: 'What plans are you making in preparation for your home in eternity? Where is your treasure stored?' Onesimus, my neighbour, would pop round my door and remark cheerfully, 'Remember the light is getting brighter every day.'

Before I slept that night, I remember thinking that we had met the devil head-on before we even reached Kampala. In the course of conversation our passenger had turned to Janani and remarked, 'You and Festo must choose your words more carefully.' He was referring to Festo's sermon earlier in the day. The devil wished to sow seeds of fear in our hearts by suggesting that we should dilute the truth.

A few days later, during the early hours of Saturday, 5th February, armed men raided Janani's house. I was wandering round the market when I first heard the rumour. Later I heard the full story from Mary and some of the children. 'They ate some of our bananas,' Phebe told me, rather enjoying the drama. At one thirty in the morning, Janani

6 79

had heard the dog barking wildly and the fence being broken down. Always on the alert, he crept downstairs to see what was happening. As he gently pulled back the curtain on the front door, he saw a man, badly beaten and cut about the face, whom he recognised at once as Ben Ongom, a business man from Lira in the north. Janani assumed he was in some kind of danger, needing help. 'We've come, Archbishop, we've come, let us in,' he called out.

Janani opened the door. Immediately three armed men sprang to attack, cocking their rifles and pushing him by force back into the dining-room, demanding, 'Show us the arms.' Their leader, who was dressed in red and spoke in Arabic, pressed his rifle into Janani's stomach, while another man searched him from head to foot. 'Take us to the bed-room, quickly,' demanded the man in red. The men made a thorough search of the upper rooms, pulling out mattresses, looking under beds, climbing into cupboards, searching through suitcases. One of them found some soap. 'Leave the soap, we are looking for arms,' shouted their leader. Mercifully the younger children slept throughout.

'What is all this about?' Janani asked. Ben Ongom explained. 'Twenty-two cases of arms were brought into the country: half were found at my house, and I am going to die for involving myself in politics. The remaining cases are still missing. We've searched Olobo's place, where they should have been, but they were not there. I thought they might be with Olobo's relative, but we found nothing when we searched his house. Then I had an idea that since he knew you, he might have brought them here. Please help us. Show us where they are hidden. If the arms are not in your house, tell us the location of any Acholi or Langi homes on Namirembe so that they may be searched.'

Janani replied: 'I did not come to Namirembe for the Acholi or the Langi. I was called by God to serve Uganda, Rwanda, Burundi and Boga-Zaire. There are no arms here. Our house is God's house. We pray for the President. We pray for the security forces. We preach the gospel. That is our work, not keeping arms to overthrow the government.' But the search continued – in the kitchen, in the store, the men thrusting their hands down into sacks of millet, sim-sim and groundnuts. 'Open the chapel,' they demanded. But they found nothing, not even under the holy table.

Eventually they grew tired and asked someone to open the gate for them. Mary retorted angrily, 'Go the way you came, through the broken fence.' But Janani said, 'No, we are Christians. We have clean hearts and as a witness to our belief we will open the gate for you.'

As word got around, everyone was shaken by this incident. For months past the security forces had raided, robbed, arrested and murdered innocent people in the name of the government but to attack the head of the church seemed incredible. People in trouble had always turned to Janani, sought his help. Where was their hope now? Suddenly it became clear that no man was safe. The government was saying, in effect : 'We can do anything.'

One of the first people to call on Janani and comfort him after the raid on his house was Cardinal Nsubuga. It was he who suggested another joint meeting of bishops similar to the one held at Lweza to draft a joint letter to the government underlining once more their stand against the anarchy in Uganda. Since the Catholic bishops were meeting on Tuesday, he said, they and the Anglicans could discuss together the raid on Janani's house and the other distressing matter, the loss of cars. He told Janani that in less than a month, sixty cars belonging to the Catholic Church had been taken at gun point. Some of the drivers were dead, others badly injured.

On the Sunday afternoon, just before the telephone lines were cut, telegrams summoning all the Anglican bishops to Kampala were sent. By lunch time on Tuesday, eight had arrived, including Bishop Okoth of Bukedi, who was able to tell the others of his arrest on the night of that same Saturday, after armed men had searched his house looking for arms. He had told the soldiers who arrested him : 'If it is death for me, it is the gateway to the Lord. If life, I will continue preaching the gospel.' At one point one of the men had shouted, 'There are many people here.' The bishop told them, 'Take a lamp, go and see.' They came back and reported they had found only cows. They took him by car as far as Jinja, but later released him with a caution not to tell anyone what had happened. 'Go on working normally,' they had ordered him. But the bishop had replied, 'These are not normal times. If you suspect me, a man dealing in spiritual matters, what of others?'

Now the bishops were determined to make a stand. They decided, before meeting the Catholics, to have their own policy clear; to put their own house in order. So they agreed to draw up a comprehensive statement of their own concern for the church and for the people whom they served. At Bweranyangi, Bishop Festo had concluded his sermon with a short story which I failed to understand at the time, but much later, I did understand it. It was about a ram and a hyena. One day the ram challenged the hyena to test his strength in a wrestling match. The contest began. Over and over again the ram threw the hyena on the ground. Each time the hyena meekly counted 'one' and got up again. Over and over again he was thrown. 'One,' gasped the hyena. Finally the inevitable happened, and the ram killed the hyena. 'I hope,' said Bishop Festo, 'that we Ugandans will remember how to count.' He continued : 'The hyena lost his life because he failed to do his arithmetic.'

The bishops, when they met on that Tuesday afternoon, 8th February, were determined to do their arithmetic correctly. The President and his Muslim entourage had thrown the people of Uganda on to the ground over and over again. Each time they had meekly risen to their feet without recounting any of their past sufferings. This time the bishops resolved to write a strong memorandum to the President expressing their grievances at the way the country was being run.

Memoranda had been written in the past but this one was different. It was frank, forthright and bold. 'Every phrase must pierce the heart,' Bishop Festo told the meeting. In it the bishops made clear to Amin their deep concern for 'the people we serve under your care'. They told him how insecure and disturbed citizens felt when security officers deviated from established procedures of law and order, and insisted that when the government needed to search the house of a top religious leader 'he should have been approached in broad daylight by responsible senior officers fully identified in conformity with his position in society'. To search a man's house at gunpoint deep in the night, the bishops said, as had been done with Archbishop Luwum and Bishop Okoth, 'leaves us without words'.

They were speaking not only for themselves, they said, but for every ordinary Christian. 'The gun whose muzzle has been pressed against the Archbishop's stomach, the gun which has been used to search the Bishop of Bukedi's house, is a gun which is being pointed at every Christian in the church.' They continued: 'The security of the ordinary Christian has been in jeopardy for quite a long time ... We have buried many who have died as a result of being shot and there are many more whose bodies have not been found, yet their disappearance is connected with the activities of some members of the security forces.' They told the President: 'We can give concrete evidence of what is happening because widows and orphans are members of our church.'

The bishops mentioned other frustrations: preferential treatment of the Muslims; the war against the educated 'which is forcing many of our people to run away from this country in spite of what the country had paid to educate them'; the confiscation of private property, such as cars, by the military; the excessive power granted to the State Research officers to arrest and kill at will.

They no longer hinted but stated clearly that the President had surrounded himself with foreigners who had no interest in Uganda, its citizens or their property. 'While you, Your Excellency, have stated on the national radio that your government is not under any foreign influence, and that your decisions are guided by your defence council and cabinet, the general trend of things in Uganda has created a feeling that the affairs of our nation are being directed by outsiders who do not have the welfare of the country and the value of the lives and properties of Ugandans at heart.'

They registered their shock when they had heard the President saying over the radio on Christmas Day that some of the bishops preached bloodshed. 'We waited anxiously to be called to clarify such a serious situation, but all in vain ... we are ready to come to you whenever there are matters that concern the church and the nation. You have only got to call us.' The bishops expressed their sorrow that the President was no longer available for consultation. 'This used not to be so, Your Excellency, when you freely moved amongst us and we freely came to you.'

As the bishops sat together in fellowship they encouraged each other. They resolved on this occasion not to work through any government department but to seek an audience with the President direct. Eight bishops were not enough: every bishop must be present when they read their memorandum to Amin. So cars were sent to collect those who remained. By Thursday afternoon all had arrived except three: two were out of the country and one assistant bishop remained in his diocese

Janani had shown a copy of the draft memorandum to Cardinal Nsubuga. There was now no mention of a joint meeting. Janani told his bishops that the Cardinal was willing to write a covering letter supporting the memorandum, but that the Catholics felt they could not sign it, since it had been written by the Church of Uganda bishops and dealt with matters affecting their church, namely the raid on the Archbishop's house and on that of the Bishop of Bukedi. The document referred only generally to the matters that were of concern to both churches. The Catholic bishops suggested various amendments and these were incorporated into the text.

After the Thursday's meeting of the bishops, I typed and duplicated many copies of the memorandum. All the copies were signed personally by the Archbishop and the fifteen bishops who were present in Kampala.

On Friday morning, 11th February, the bishops met again. I was reminded of the occasions when Jesus sat in fellowship with his disciples, though, at the time, no one thought that this would be the last occasion Janani would sit with his bishops. He shared with them a Bible passage he had read with his wife that morning. It was the story of the disciples trying to cross the stormy Sea of Galilee alone while the Master was praying in the hills: 'And when evening came, the boat was out at sea, and he was alone on the land. And he saw that they were making headway painfully . . . ' Janani turned to his bishops and said: 'The Lord has seen us in the past four days making headway painfully. But I see the way ahead very clearly. There are storms, waves, wind and danger, but I see the road clearly.'

Although the bishops had asked for an appointment to see the President, there was still no word from him. On Saturday about half of them returned to their dioceses for Sunday, while the remainder stayed on in Kampala.

Sunday passed. On Monday, 14th February, the President sent for the Archbishop alone. Mary tried to dissuade him from going. He told her, 'I will go. Even if he kills me, my blood will save the nation.' Mary went with him to State House in Entebbe. Over a cup of tea Amin accused Janani of plotting with Obote to overthrow the government and he claimed that cases of arms had been found by children near his house. The allegations were repeated on Radio Uganda and on television that night and in the official newspaper, *Voice of Uganda*, the following day. No mention was made of the memorandum from the bishops. That same day, while Janani was with the President, the memorandum was delivered personally to all cabinet ministers, religious leaders and to the secretary of the defence council.

Janani drafted a reply refuting Amin's allegations. He asked about the arms allegedly found near his residence: 'Your Excellency said that arms "were found near my residence". That is not clear enough, might I ask where exactly? If so, who brought them there? When these were found, since it was near our residence and I was searched at gun point for them, why was I not brought to witness the discovery?'

Janani reminded the President that many Ugandans had fled the country or had been killed on baseless allegations. He concluded: 'I would like the whole world to know that I am innocent of this serious matter of state security.' But the letter was never sent. Events moved too quickly.

Late on Tuesday afternoon word reached the provincial office that the President had called a meeting for nine thirty next day, Wednesday, 16th February, at the International Conference Centre in Kampala. He wanted to address all government officials, members of the armed forces, ambassadors and religious leaders.

Our centenary co-ordinator felt that Janani should not attend the meeting alone. He drove through the night and collected all the Church of Uganda bishops on the eastern side of Uganda and brought them to Kampala. There are many who will never forget his act of charity, his courage and forethought.

I was not there as the last act of the drama unfolded. I had earlier arranged to go to Kisumu in Kenya for the weekend and though I was loath to leave, Janani encouraged me. By the time I returned to Kampala a few days later, Janani was dead.

He had arrived with six of his bishops early that Wednesday morning to find a vast assembly arrayed to meet them in the spacious grounds of the Nile Mansions Hotel outside the Conference Centre. There were several hundred troops, a large group of governors, administrators, diplomats, heads of departments, and all religious leaders, including Cardinal Nsubuga. On display stood suitcases packed tightly with Chinese automatic weapons, thousands of rounds of ammunition and hundreds of hand grenades. Like strangers in an alien land, they felt themselves hemmed in by evil on every side. 'You could see the hatred in the men's eyes,' Bishop Festo told me afterwards. 'We were marked men dressed in our purple bishops' robes.' The sun blazed down. They wanted to move into the shade, but the soldiers roughly ordered them back.

The Vice-President was in charge of the staged trial. He ordered a prisoner under arrest, Aballa Anywui, former Chairman of Uganda's Public Service Commission, to read a long memorandum allegedly drawn up by the deposed President Obote. The so-called memorandum suggested ways of mobilising opposition to the Amin regime and said arms could be shipped to Uganda through the Anglican Bishop Okoth on Kenya's border. Okoth, said the memorandum, could then pass the arms on to the Archbishop.

Bishop Festo stood next to Janani. He told me that when Janani heard his name mentioned, he made no reply, merely shook his head in denial. He whispered to Bishop Festo, 'They are going to kill me. I am not afraid.' In some ways there was a similarity with the trial of Christ himself, whom Janani had always sought to follow. 'As a sheep before its shearers is dumb, so he opened not his mouth' (Isa. 53.7).

The Vice-President insinuated that the church leaders had been meddling in government affairs, considering themselves above the law. Finally he shouted, 'What shall we do with these traitors?'

'Kill them, kill them now,' cried the soldiers in response.

'Put up your hands, all you who want them shot in public.' All the soldiers put up their hands.

'Put up your hands, all you who don't want them to be shot.' Not a hand was raised.

The bishops thought they might be arrested straight away, and that there could even be a public shooting.

'No, they will be given a fair trial by military tribunal.'

The Vice-President dismissed the crowd. Cardinal Nsubuga and his chaplain were told to go home. The other religious leaders, diplomats, government officers and senior military officers were asked to go into the conference centre. Here the bishops were ushered into a side room along with the Muslim mufti, with a security officer in plain clothes to guard them. They sat there, slowly realising that they were virtually prisoners. The minutes ticked by. They could hear the applause and shouts in the background. 'Now you can go home and do your work,' the guard told them, when he heard the order of dismissal. But suddenly he barked fresh orders: 'You, Luwum, are wanted in that room by the President.' Bishop Silvanus Wani, of Amin's own Kakwa tribe, chaplain of the armed forces, Dean of the Province and later elected Archbishop, tried to follow, but they pushed him back, saying, 'We don't need you. His Excellency wants to talk with Luwum.'

Janani turned and smiled: 'I can see the hand of the Lord in this,' he said. It was his farewell. They never saw him again.

All afternoon Bishop Festo and Bishop Silvanus waited in the scorching sun by Janani's car. At intervals they would enquire, 'Will the Archbishop be long? When can we expect him to join us?' Always the terse reply was, 'He will come later. He is busy with His Excellency.'

At five o'clock the two bishops were turned away at gun point. With heavy hearts they drove back to join the other bishops waiting at the Archbishop's house. When Mary realised her husband had not returned with them, she became hysterical. She jumped into the car and ordered their driver to take her to the conference centre. 'I want to go in and find my husband,' she said to the guards at the gate. For answer the soldiers pointed their guns at them, and the driver was almost shot before they turned back. It is probable that by then Janani was already dead.

'There is a rumour,' writes Bishop Festo, 'that they were trying to make him sign a confession, which he would not do. We were also told that he was praying aloud for his captors when he died. We have talked with eyewitnesses who claim they saw him shot, and to others who saw the bodies in the morgue with bullet wounds. Evidence suggests that he was shot at six o'clock.' (*I Love Idi Amin*)

In the evening Radio Uganda announced that Janani and two cabinet ministers, Erinayo Oryema and Charles Oboth Ofumbi, had been arrested. The following morning, just after the provincial office staff had finished praying, their hearts deeply troubled, a woman rushed in, flourishing a newspaper with its terrible headlines: ARCHBISHOP AND TWO MINISTERS DIE IN MOTOR ACCIDENT.

The circumstances surrounding Janani's death will probably never be entirely discovered. But it is known that he was shot, twice through the chest and through the mouth.

10. An Empty Grave

On the Thursday morning, I arrived back from Kenya. Our journey had been uneventful. On the surface everything appeared quiet and normal. There were no road blocks. But the scene outside the provincial office was far from normal. Small groups of people were huddled together, and no one was smiling. They told me that the worst had happened, and Janani had been killed. I was not really surprised. The Lord had already prepared me. The night before I drove back to Kampala, he had revealed to me, so vividly, the crucifixion. It was as if he was saying, 'I am innocent, but they nailed me to the cross. My son, Janani, is innocent, but they are going to kill him. He is following in my footsteps.'

When the public learned that the Archbishop had been killed, a deathly hush settled over Kampala. Even the birds seemed to stop singing. Words were useless. I found myself wandering up the hill towards Namirembe Cathedral. Someone was playing the organ: the hymn 'O Jesus I have promised' echoed round the cathedral. I knelt to pray: 'O Jesus, *I have* promised to serve you to the end. Thank you that Janani was able to serve you to the end. Help me too.'

Later a group of us went to a service and heard the apostle Paul's words, 'Vengeance is mine, I will repay, says the Lord . . . ' (Rom. 12.9). I remembered my conversation with Bishop Festo that afternoon. He knew I had no words, only tears. He said, 'Let's pray,' and began: 'O Loving Father, help us to forgive the men who murdered Janani. Help us to pray that your Holy Spirit will convict them, that they will repent and be saved by your cleansing blood.'

For the rest of the day we just sat around, unable to comprehend what had happened. That night security men began systematically to raid the houses belonging to the church on Namirembe Hill, one of the Anglican Church's sacred places, the hill of peace. Struck by a remark Bishop Festo had made earlier in the day, 'We lost Janani because we allowed him to be isolated', we moved in together — the group of us living on our small compound, determined that when the soldiers came, they would find us praising the Lord, and singing the *balokole* hymn:

> Even at the point of death
> Jesus alone satisfies;
> I will rest in Him.
> Jesus alone satisfies;
> Even in great sorrow,
> At the point of death,
> I will still sing,
> 'Jesus satisfies'.

On the following days the government told so many lies. Their story was that the Archbishop and the two cabinet ministers, Charles Oboth Ofumbi and Erinayo Oryema, had been killed on their way for questioning when they attempted to overpower the driver and escape. Their car had crashed during the struggle and this was how they died. No one, of course, believed it. One edition of the *Voice of Uganda* printed a photograph of a car involved in a head-on collision; the following day's edition showed a car involved in a side-on collision. Both cars were recognised as having been concerned in crashes previously. They had been seen lying in a garage some days before.

If the Archbishop had really died in the way the authorities pretended, why did they hide the body? The bishops tried in vain to claim it for burial at Namirembe. The grave was dug. At midday on Friday, the bishops were told that the body had been taken north for private burial near the Archbishop's home at Mucwini.

Mary and the children were virtually prisoners in their home in Kampala. Hundreds of people came to offer her words of comfort, to sit with her for a little while. We were warned to be careful, since there were security men mingling with the mourners in the Archbishop's own sitting-room, noting carefully who was there, and trying to pick up snatches of conversation. Later, Mary and the children were able to escape to Kenya.

A funeral service with mourners from many countries had been planned for Sunday, 20th February, in Namirembe Cathedral. Archbishop Olang' of Kenya had been asked to preach. A large delegation was gathered in Nairobi, including church leaders from the Sudan, Nigeria, Liberia, Lesotho, Cameroun and Kenya. Together with Dr Leslie Brown, Uganda's first Archbishop, they were ready to cross the border, when the memorial service in Namirembe Cathedral was cancelled. Instead, they held their memorial service for Janani in Kenya, in All Saints Cathedral, Nairobi.

In Uganda that Sunday morning, the radio told us that there would be no special prayers about the dead Archbishop. But this announcement did not deter thousands of people from attending the usual service of mattins in Namirembe Cathedral. Tears flowed easily at this stage. A group of us who had been taking a service elsewhere made our way up the hill to join the thousands already packed into the cathedral. Someone made room for us on a bench outside. As the service came to its end, the unusually long procession moved slowly out, followed by the congregation. No one dispersed. Everyone stood as if they were waiting for something to happen, for someone to say something. Then suddenly voices began to sing, over and over again the hymn sung by the first Ugandan martyrs:

> Daily, daily sing the praises
> Of the City God hath made;
> In the beauteous Field of Eden
> Its foundation-stones are laid.
>
> O, that I had wings of angels
> Here to spread and heavenward fly;
> I would seek the gates of Sion
> Far beyond the starry sky!
>
> In the midst of that dear City
> Christ is reigning on His seat,
> And the angels swing their censers
> In a ring about His feet.

We rejoice at that fair City
Which our Saviour has prepared,
And we walk on earth as pilgrims;
With the saints our call is shared.

Grant, O Lord, our eyes be open
Here to see our Saviour King,
And our hearts be ever eager
Him to hear, His praise to sing.

Thus, Janani, our beloved Archbishop, was proclaimed the
first martyr of the second century of the Church of Uganda,
following the steps of those earlier martyrs who had died
so soon after its birth. The centenary had been launched
with the blood of Janani, led like a lamb to the slaughter,
following our Lord and Master, Jesus Christ, along the same
road as Yusufu, the youngest of the first three boy martyrs.

Then our eyes fell on the empty grave, a gaping hole in
the earth. The words of the angel to the two women seeking
Jesus's body flashed into our minds. 'Why do you seek the
living among the dead?' Namirembe Hill resounded with
the song that the *balokole* have taken as their own,
Tukutendereza Yesu:

Glory, glory, hallelujah!
Glory, glory to the Lamb!
Oh, the cleansing blood has reached me!
Glory, glory to the Lamb!

We came away from the service praising, healed by the
revelation of the empty grave. We greeted each other, using
the words of the old Easter greeting: 'Christ is risen' – 'He
is risen indeed!' Archbishop Sabiti spoke to me briefly as I
was leaving: 'Why are we bothering about the body?
Janani went straight to heaven.'

At our Sunday evening fellowship meeting there were
many testimonies. 'When I heard the Archbishop was dead,
I wanted to slaughter the men who had killed him. Now the
Lord is convicting me to pray for his murderers that they
will repent and be saved by the cleansing blood of Christ.'
And from someone else: 'I know Christ has risen. He healed
me today through the power of the resurrection.'

The resurrection is the heart of the gospel we proclaim and because I have tasted the reality of the resurrection, I know I must continue telling others, 'Christ lives.'